# the ALGONQUIN

# ROUND TABLE

# NEW YORK  a historical guide

Also by Kevin C. Fitzpatrick:

*Under the Table: A Dorothy Parker Cocktail Guide*

*A Journey into Dorothy Parker's New York*

As Editor

*Dorothy Parker Complete Broadway, 1918–1923*

*The Lost Algonquin Round Table:*
*Humor, Fiction, Journalism, Criticism, and Poetry*
*from America's Most Famous Literary Circle*
*(with Nat Benchley)*

# the ALGONQUIN
# ROUND TABLE
# NEW YORK  a historical guide

### KEVIN C. FITZPATRICK

with a foreword by Anthony Melchiorri

Guilford, Connecticut

An imprint of Rowman & Littlefield

Distributed by NATIONAL BOOK NETWORK

British Library Cataloguing-in-Publication Information Available

**Library of Congress Cataloging-in-Publication Data**

Fitzpatrick, Kevin C., 1966-
  The Algonquin Round Table New York : a historical guide / Kevin C. Fitzpatrick ; with a foreword by Anthony Melchiorri.
       pages cm
  Summary: "Explores the shadowy speakeasies, majestic hotels, glittering theaters, and other locations frequented by the legends of the Algonquin Round Table"—Provided by publisher.
  Includes bibliographical references and index.
  ISBN 978-1-4930-0757-8 (hardback)
  1. Authors, American—Homes and haunts—New York (State)—New York. 2. Authors, American—20th century—Biography. 3. Algonquin Round Table. 4. Intellectuals—New York (State)—New York—History—20th century. 5. Intellectuals—New York (State)—New York—Biography. 6. New York (N.Y.)—Intellectual life—20th century. I. Title.
  PS129.F58 2015
  810.9'0052—dc23

                                                             2014037678

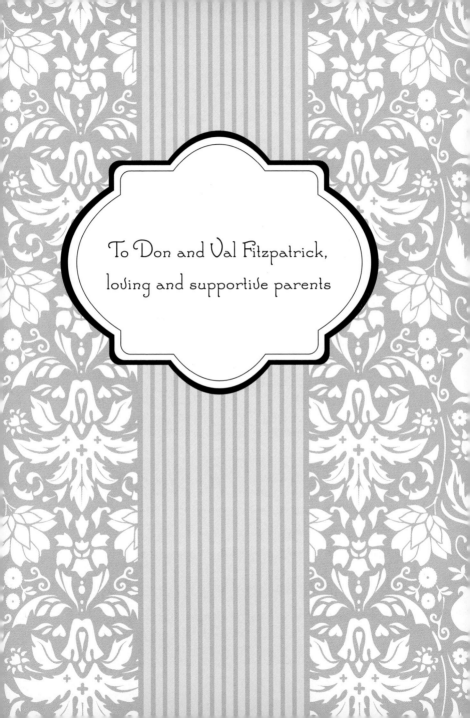

To Don and Val Fitzpatrick,
loving and supportive parents

# CONTENTS

# FOREWORD

A New York City legend in the heart of the Theater District, the Algonquin Hotel is over one hundred years old but as spry as a teenager. Better yet, the spirit of the Round Table is alive and well, forever smiling down on all who pass through the lobby.

In June 1919 some of Gotham's most famous, talented, opinionated, and outlandishly funny writers and critics met one day for lunch. They had such a good time that they met again the next day—and the day after. Their number included columnists, critics, humorists, playwrights, publicists, publishers, and sportswriters. Joining the ranks were occasional friends and lovers, among them actors and novelists of note. But the queen of the prom was Dorothy Parker: critic, poet, short-story writer, and screenwriter. She was everything the hotel was, and is, and these days, the two are inseparable. Both she and the hotel are brilliant, moody, genius, complex, tragic, and,

Anthony Melchiorri. ◆ ◆ ◆

yes, even funny. She and her peers came to "The Gonk" for lunch six times a week for the next ten years.

Like any hotel, the Algonquin will give you a place to sleep, a bathroom, and something to eat. The rooms are no more special than in most boutique hotels. They're comfortable, sure, but they're still hotel rooms. Except calling the Algonquin just another hotel would be like calling Dorothy Parker just another writer.

I was lucky enough to be general manager of the hotel for two years—a dream job in the business—but I came to the Algonquin kicking and screaming. When I arrived in 2004, the place was past its prime, and it looked like a career killer. The risk was huge. On my first day, I walked in thinking that with a good plan and the help of longtime employees, I could rely on history to bring back the hotel. What I didn't realize was the depth of that history and the emotional connection that people have with the place.

The lobby was cool before cool became synonymous with hotels. In fact, this is where the "social lobby" came into being. It served as a living room for actors, dancers, directors, painters, politicians, and writers, constantly stopping by to schmooze or just hang out. On just one Saturday night during my tenure there, Andrea Marcovicci performed in the Oak Room; Tony Bennett sat in the audience; in the lobby, writer George Will was talking with friends; and Carson Daly was in the Blue Bar trying not to be noticed. Edward Albee, Christine Ebersole, Debbie Harry, Donna Karan, Martin McDonagh, Isaac Mizrahi, Cynthia Nixon, and John Patrick Shanley all made appearances, as did many more, when I was running the hotel.

The Gonk became the first hotel to use electronic keys. It developed the first hotel marketing campaign aimed exclusively toward women. It used the first red rope for crowd control. It was also home to the Algonquin Cocktail, consisting of two shots of rye, one of dry vermouth, and another of pineapple juice. The Vicious Circle was a martini crowd. That's what they drank before lunch, during lunch, and sometimes instead of lunch. Of course during Prohibition the hotel was "officially" dry—which may explain why they met here all the time. As Dorothy Parker purportedly wrote:

*I love a martini—*
*But two at the most.*
*Three, I'm under the table;*
*Four, I'm under the host.*

Ironically, she wasn't much of a martini drinker herself; she preferred the brown stuff: A whiskey sour was more her style. When my team and I were working on a renovation and marketing campaign for the hotel, PR consultant Carla Caccavale said, "Here's a place famous for martinis, so why not reinvent the Algonquin Martini?"—which we did.

We added another noteworthy first to the Algonquin's list of achievements: the world's first $10,000 martini. Early on, I noticed that many couples were getting engaged in our lobby, so I thought, why not make it easier for them? I hired a staff jeweler, who meets with the future groom to pick a diamond. The jeweler then oversees the setting, and when it's ready, the couple, along with their family and friends, just happens to stop by for a drink. We deliver our famous martini to the unsuspecting bride-to-be, who discovers an engagement ring at the bottom of her glass. No other martini has produced as many howls of surprise, fits of laughter, rounds of applause, or tears of joy.

We updated the restaurant menus to reflect the Round Table years as well, thanks to owner and first general manager, Frank Case. In the Forties, he authored a book called *Feeding the Lions*, a reference to the literary lions who made the Gonk their second home. In it, he documented the food served during the height of their fame. All that the head chef and I had to do was sit down and modernize those famous dishes.

But the Gonk wasn't just a writers' spot; it was also a show business hangout. In the past, many great hotels had show rooms. I wanted to bring back that touch of history, so we made the Oak Room the Algonquin's show room. Peter Cincotti, Harry Connick Jr., Diana Krall, and Maude Maggart have all played there. You could even say that the hotel has its own Oscar. The Round Table was the subject of *The Ten-Year Lunch*, which won the 1987 Academy Award for best documentary.

The Oscar is special, but how many hotels have a legendary house cat? At the Algonquin, Matilda rules the roost. Some even think that Dorothy Parker's spirit lives on in her. Believe what you like, but I wouldn't be at all surprised if Mrs. Parker's spirit does reside somewhere in the hotel, in one form or another, because nothing surprises me about the Algonquin. There's no other place like it in the world, and I'm humbled to have walked in the footsteps of those visionaries.

—Anthony Melchiorri, creator and host of the
Travel Channel's *Hotel Impossible* and former
general manager of the Algonquin Hotel

——————— ♦ ♦ ♦ ———————

Silly of me to blame it on dates,
but so it happened to be.
Dammit, it was the Twenties, and
we had to be smarty.

—Dorothy Parker

——————— ♦ ♦ ♦ ———————

Broadway had a big influence on the Algonquin Round Table. ◆ ◆ ◆

# "WHY DON'T WE DO THIS EVERY DAY?"

New York City's Jazz Age and the Legends It Spawned

*Nothing is more responsible for the good old days than a bad memory.*

—FRANKLIN P. ADAMS

On Christmas Day, 1923, readers of the *New York Times* opened their papers and learned that the poor were not being forgotten. A group of philanthropists had organized more than five thousand yuletide deliveries by borrowing limousines belonging to the upper class. Commander in chief of the operation, Neysa McMein—whom the page-one *Times* story dubbed "Santa Claus's traffic manager"— finagled chauffeured cars from financier Bernard Baruch, composer Irving Berlin, and *New York World* editor Herbert Bayard Swope to deliver toys and turkeys to the Lower East Side.

A decade earlier, Marjorie Moran McMein, an unknown commercial artist from Quincy, Illinois, had about as much chance of making the front page of the *Times* as the tooth fairy. She had come to Manhattan by way of Chicago, but in a few short years had become the most sought-after magazine illustrator in the business. She was following the path of a special clique that formed in the months after the Great War. Coming to New York to reinvent herself, she took on the fanciful moniker of "Neysa" on the advice of a numerologist—or from a racehorse, depending on who tells the story.

Neysa McMein hailed from Quincy, Illinois. ◆ ◆ ◆

McMein was in good company that holiday. Franklin Pierce Adams, also a native of the Prairie State, was the most popular columnist in the city, and known by his initials, F.P.A. Robert Benchley, a peripatetic writer and humorist from Worcester, Massachusetts, was launching himself from publishing to talking pictures. Jane Grant, a Kansas farmer's daughter who came to the city with dreams of becoming a singer, became the first female beat reporter for the *Times*. McMein's neighbor at **57 West 57th Street,** Dorothy Parker, grew up on Manhattan's Upper West Side, talked her way into a job at *Vogue,* and had become the most-quoted woman in the nation. Rounding out the holiday cadre was Alexander Woollcott, a rotund drama critic from a commune near Red Bank, New Jersey, who invariably swept into Broadway theaters wearing a silk top hat and cape.

But why would the newspaper of record write about a midwestern painter renowned for depicting fetching women for magazine covers? It wasn't for McMein's professional reputation alone; it was also because of the company she kept. For the past four and half years, she and her nearly inseparable group of friends had eaten lunch together, held marathon poker parties, collaborated on hit shows, and turned out best-selling novels. In the early evenings, they visited her art studio. By June 1919, they had become darlings of the press. When they became regulars at a hotel restaurant on the edge of the Theater District, the proprietor gave the gang a dedicated table—large, circular, just for them—that gave them their collective nickname: the Algonquin Round Table. They called themselves the Vicious Circle, and the group made headlines every single day.

"The world in which we moved was small, but it was churning with a dynamic group of young people," said Marc Connelly, a transplant from McKeesport, Pennsylvania, who wrote hit plays with his Algonquin friends. Connelly stood among the many journalists who ditched jobs at newspapers and magazines to become playwrights, screenwriters, producers, and directors. Publicists, editors, cartoonists, and actors joined them, and they all found friendship and encouragement at the round table in the Rose Room at the hotel.

"I had been graciously included in the early spontaneous gatherings," recalled Peggy Wood, a sleek Broadway actress from Brooklyn.

> It was a lively bunch, all in the beginnings of their careers, eager, witty, and alert. There was no set time for lunch and no closed shop on the membership.... Between the hours of one and two-thirty there might be six or sixteen around the board. Once a guest was brought he was at liberty to come again as often as he wished by himself, but I can't recall that anybody ever barged in under his own steam. There wasn't any rule about it, there weren't any rules about anything, but somehow there were never any gate-crashers.

When the Round Table took off in the summer of 1919, Connelly was twenty-eight years old, and Wood, twenty-seven, ages that matched most of the group. The dean of the gathering, F.P.A., was pushing thirty-seven. Together, they came to represent all that was racy, refined, and romantic in the era of the "smart set" of Manhattan. The New York City they inhabited was a shadow of what it is today, but even while the Round Table was in full swing, a cultural sea change was remaking the metropolis. Nothing ever stays the same in New York City, and the Vicious Circle was in the thick of it all, experiencing and observing the city's dizzying highs and crushing lows.

## Swelling, Selling, and Scandal: New York, 1900–1919

In 1900, New York was a gritty and dangerous place. In the harbor, the new immigration station on Ellis Island was expanded, and in December of that year a new fireproof main building was dedicated. Within sight of the Statue of Liberty, the beautiful Beaux Arts–style building with soaring redbrick towers became a symbol for generations. Immigrants arrived by the shipload and poured into a city run by corrupt politicians, filling overcrowded firetrap tenements that had shocking sanitary conditions. Like most big cities of the era, vice was common. New York had 25,000 prostitutes; their come-on was, "It costs a dollar, and I've got the room."

The population of greater New York reached 3.4 million people—over a third foreign-born—making it the largest city in the Western Hemisphere. But vestiges of the city's Colonial past still lingered: Some two thousand private farms still existed within New York City at the turn of the twentieth century, some stretching for twenty-five acres. Residents filled up the five boroughs, united only in 1898. Despite hardships, many of them lived comfortably, however. A full meal in a restaurant cost, on average, just 15 cents. A six-room apartment on West 98th Street rented for about $22 to

A taxi crashed into subway excavation work on Seventh Avenue in 1915. ◆ ◆ ◆

$28 per month. Broadway fans had eighty stages to entertain them; streetcars cost a nickel; and elevated train lines sailed above Second, Third, Sixth, and Ninth Avenues.

Meanwhile, commerce and industry were going pell-mell. About 47 percent of all US foreign trade passed through the busy Port of New York. On March 24, 1900, excavation for the new subway network began at the corner of Bleecker and Greene Streets for what would become one of the busiest subway systems in the world, carrying more than a billion riders annually. Almost eight thousand laborers worked for 20 cents an hour to dig the subway tunnels.

During the first two decades of the twentieth century, the future members of the Algonquin Round Table converged on New York City. Some, such as F.P.A., left successful careers for more-promising ones. F. P. A. had worked in Chicago before joining the New York *Morning Telegraph* in 1903, and then the *New-York Tribune* ("First to Last—The Truth"). Marc Connelly worked as a reporter for the *Pittsburgh Gazette Times* before bolting for the New York *Morning Telegraph* in 1917. Milwaukee journalist Edna Ferber rocketed to national fame as a young short-story writer. (President Theodore Roosevelt was a fan of her Emma McChesney tales.)

It didn't matter if your skills were with a typewriter or tap shoes. Jobs were plentiful in New York then. The city had sixteen daily newspapers published in morning and evening editions. Nearly eighty "legitimate" theaters made up Broadway, and there were dozens of burlesque and vaudeville houses. When financial mismanagement forced Joseph Pulitzer's sons to close the *New York World* in 1931, Frank Sullivan wrote, "When I die I want to go wherever the *World* has gone, and work on it again."

The dominant event of this era was World War I. Patriotism reached an all-time high, and volunteers poured into New York to sign up. For the journalists among the future group, there was no

In 1932, the Central Park Reservoir dried up and squatters built a shantytown. ◆ ◆ ◆

escaping impending American involvement in the war in Europe. Twenty-nine-year-old Heywood Broun, a sportswriter turned editorial writer, begged to go. He took his new wife, Ruth Hale, a fellow writer and ardent feminist. F.P.A. was commissioned a captain and sailed for France. Also shipping out for duty were Private Harold W. Ross, an itinerant newspaperman, and Private Alexander Woollcott, who took a leave of absence from the *Times* to join a local hospital support unit. Jane Grant signed up with an entertainment outfit to get passage to the combat zone and joined the party. Herman Mankiewicz, just twenty years old when he enlisted in the Marines, came out an officer. When the war ended, he became a foreign correspondent for the *World*. Laurence Stallings was also in the Marines, and grievously wounded.

# From the Army to the Algonquin

Adams and Ross served on *Stars and Stripes.* ◆ ◆ ◆

The Great War featured many innovations never seen before in international armed conflict: airplanes, blimps, poison gas, tanks. Add to that list one other new creation: an official newspaper for the troops. The US Army published *Stars and Stripes* weekly for the doughboys, and from 1918 to 1919, three future members of the Round Table worked on the paper. Franklin P. Adams was sent to Paris as an army columnist, but he didn't have much to do—unlike in New York, where he penned the city's most popular column. Harold Ross had been a freelance reporter, working coast to coast on a string of papers. A natural-born editor, he cut his teeth on *Stars and Stripes.* The paper's staff picked him, the buck private, to be managing editor. Alexander Woollcott made sergeant while on bedpan duty in a frontline hospital unit, but he finagled a transfer to the newspaper office in the 1st arrondissement.

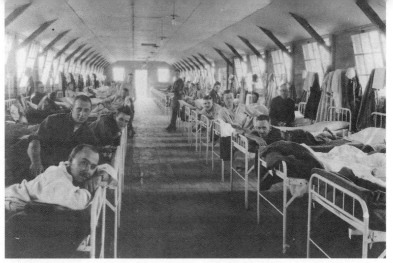

Woollcott worked in an army hospital in World War I; Sherwood and Stallings had their lives saved in one. ◆ ◆ ◆

The misfits who ended up in a war zone became friends and dined out on their war stories for decades. They started a tradition in Nini's—a small bistro on Place du Tertre in Montmartre—that they continued for twenty years in New York: marathon Saturday-night poker-and-bull sessions. In Paris they formed lifelong friendships, and the war established the backdrop to the rest of their lives.

By early 1919, the war had ended, and most of the soldiers returned home. Woollcott lingered in France as part of the Army of Occupation. When he sailed back to Manhattan and his old position as drama critic for the *Times*, F.P.A. wasted no time in ribbing him in his *Tribune* column:

> Bluff, uncouth Aleck Woollcott is back from France and in his embarrassed way stutters his elation. "Are you glad to be back?" asked *The Tribune*'s dramatic and book reviewer [Heywood Broun]. "I'll say I am," said Mr. Woollcott, blushing. The day after Sgt. Woollcott was demobilized, he met General Pershing. "He's a civilian now," said Lieutenant [Stephen] Early, who introduced Woollcott to the Commander in Chief. "He looks like a soldier to me," said the General. In Sgt. Woollcott's twenty-two months in the Army, it was the first time anybody had said anything of the kind to him.

Backstage at the Hippodrome Theatre, Murdock Pemberton spots for a chorus girl's rehearsal. ◆ ◆ ◆

The Algonquin had operated for close to twenty years before the Round Table took up residence, but the Vicious Circle didn't form inside the hotel, or even in New York. The roots of the Round Table went back to Paris. Eight of the future Algonquin friends served in uniform during World War I; several others were in France as civilians. The shared experiences of the group—working together, sharing meals, playing cards—transferred back to Manhattan when the war ended.

When soldiers returned to New York in early 1919, the 369th Regiment marched from Lower Manhattan up Fifth Avenue to Harlem, cheered by more than a million jubilant onlookers. Leading the column was James Reese Europe's jazz band, which struck up "Here Comes My Daddy Now" when it reached 110th Street. After the festivities, most of the soldier-journalists returned to their old jobs. The *Tribune* welcomed home F.P.A., who promptly returned to "The Conning Tower," his daily column, with this amusing couplet:

> *I didn't fight and I didn't shoot.*
> *But General, how I did salute!*

When Woollcott got back to the *Times*, a few Broadway publicists set events in motion that led to the formation of the Round Table. John Peter Toohey and Murdock Pemberton, friends of Woollcott's, brought him to the hotel. Pemberton worked for the **Hippodrome, 1120 Sixth Avenue,** across the street from the Algonquin. The biggest theater Broadway ever saw, boasting more than five thousand seats, The Hippodrome occupied the full span between 43rd and 44th Streets. Its water tank had swimming showgirls. Toohey was representing a rising star, playwright Eugene O'Neill, who was writing *Beyond the Horizon* for the **Morosco Theatre, 217 West 45th Street.** With two hundred shows opening each year on Broadway, getting the attention of a powerful critic like Woollcott wasn't easy. But they had an idea.

Woollcott's famous sweet tooth couldn't resist the desserts created by Sarah Victor, star of the Algonquin kitchen. The rotund critic eagerly accepted their lunch invitation. But to the publicists' dismay, Woollcott wouldn't listen to them about O'Neill. Instead, he dominated the table with war stories about Arleux, the Somme, and Ypres. His yarns began, "When I was in the theatre of war . . ." (To which publicist Arthur Samuels interrupted: "Listen, if you were ever in the theatre of war you sat in row Z on the aisle.") When the lunch ended unsuccessfully, the publicity men returned to work and formulated a plan.

## LAUNCHING THE ROUND TABLE

Using their publicity skills, the men hatched a scheme. They planned a roast for Woollcott, a welcome-home luncheon like the city had never seen. They drew the guest list from among friends and associates. Many had office jobs within easy walking distance of the hotel; the others could take the nearby Sixth Avenue elevated train.

According to Margaret Case, who grew up in the hotel and knew every member of the group, the "official" members consisted of a who's who of writing and acting. First up, the newspapermen: Franklin P. Adams, Heywood Broun, and Deems Taylor at the *Tribune*; Marc Connelly of the *Morning Telegraph*; George S. Kaufman and Woollcott at the *Times*; Frank Sullivan at the *World*; William B. Murray and John V. A. Weaver of the *Brooklyn Daily Eagle*. Beatrice Kaufman, George's wife, worked as an editor. Then their magazine friends: from *Vanity Fair*, managing editor Robert Benchley, drama critic Dorothy Parker, and writer Robert E. Sherwood; and Margaret Leech, fresh out of Vassar, from Condé Nast. Joining their ranks were Ruth Hale, who wrote book reviews and press releases; Harold Ross, who was struggling with editing work; Donald Ogden Stewart, a light comedy writer and playwright. Journalists Jane Grant, Herman J. Mankiewicz, and Laurence Stallings were overseas when the group began, and joined later.

On the Broadway side, there were press agents Murdock Pemberton, Arthur Samuels, John Peter Toohey, and David H. Wallace. Pemberton's older brother, Brock, was producing hit plays. Margalo Gillmore and Peggy Wood were Broadway stars. Artist Neysa McMein didn't visit the hotel much; the group usually visited her studio in the late afternoon for socializing. Completing the circle was novelist Edna Ferber, probably the most financially successful member of the group. Ferber claimed she was only a part-time member—and only on Saturdays—because of her writing regimen. Harpo Marx joined in 1924. Some of the members enjoyed being associated with the group; in time, others recoiled at any mention of the Round Table, considering it a frivolous period in their careers.

Woollcott was sensitive about the spelling of his name, so the invitations (none survive) that Pemberton composed for lunch made a mishmash of it. The men asked the Hippodrome scenery department to create a large banner that hung across the Algonquin dining room and misspelled Woollcott's name again. Woollcott brought Ross, his old army buddy, and introduced him to the group. About twenty friends filled up long tables in the Pergola Room (today the Oak Room) and had a smashing time. Frank Case happily hosted the group that played such a big part in the life of the city.

Nobody wrote down what was said or discussed at that very first meeting, but the mood and the fun struck a chord with the talented young New Yorkers. As they walked into the daylight of West 44th Street, someone asked, "Why don't we do this every day?"

A ritual and a legend were born.

The West 85th Street house that Heywood Broun won in a poker game became a favorite Round Table destination. ◆ ◆ ◆

# {2}

# MEET THE ROUND TABLE
## Thirty Friends Together

*No essence can be measured by a yardstick.*
—HEYWOOD BROUN

Separating fact from fiction in telling the history of the Round Table is a job for Sisyphus. "We all loved each other," Marc Connelly recalled not long before he died in 1980. "We hated to be apart. After lunch we went to somebody's house and figured out someplace to have dinner." That much is true. Otherwise, dates are sketchy. Most accounts contradict others. Biographies repeat the same anecdotes with different protagonists. Quips, quotes, and jokes are all attributed to different people. Some believe the group lasted ten years; others put it between six and eight. By the time the stock market crashed in 1929, the members of the Vicious Circle had gone their separate ways, although many stayed close friends for the rest of their lives. Here are brief biographies of the complete Algonquin Round Table.

Julius Tannen, Beatrice and George Kaufman, Atlantic City, 1925. ◆ ◆ ◆

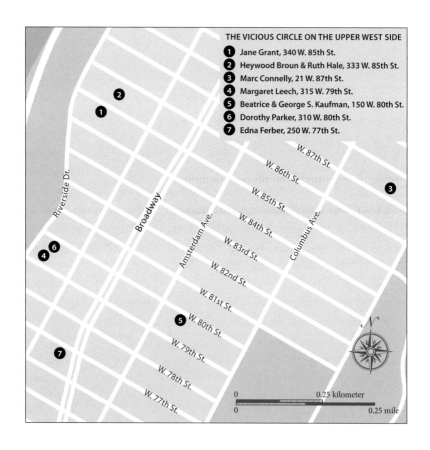

THE VICIOUS CIRCLE ON THE UPPER WEST SIDE

1  Jane Grant, 340 W. 85th St.
2  Heywood Broun & Ruth Hale, 333 W. 85th St.
3  Marc Connelly, 21 W. 87th St.
4  Margaret Leech, 315 W. 79th St.
5  Beatrice & George S. Kaufman, 150 W. 80th St.
6  Dorothy Parker, 310 W. 80th St.
7  Edna Ferber, 250 W. 77th St.

# Franklin P. Adams

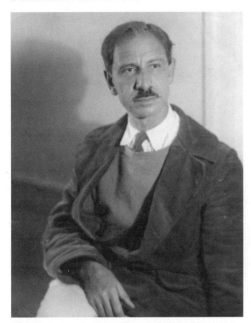

F.P.A. wrote more than two million words during his career. ◆ ◆ ◆

The dean of the Round Table and New York's most popular newspaper columnist for two generations was Franklin Pierce Adams. For nearly forty years his columns appeared in New York newspapers. His readers knew him as "F.P.A.," and he accepted submissions from readers, calling them "contribs." Landing in F.P.A.'s column was a coup. He ran early material by George S. Kaufman, James Thurber, Edna St. Vincent Millay, Deems Taylor, and E. B. White. He also included scores of poems by Dorothy Parker. ("He raised me from a couplet," she later quipped.)

Born in Chicago on November 15, 1881, the son of a dry goods merchant, Adams spent a year at the University of Michigan but withdrew after the death of his father. Following a stint in the insurance business, Adams landed a job at the *Chicago Mail*, where he wrote his first column. But he was itching to head to New York; he had his eye on a pretty actress named Minna Schwartze, two years his senior. His editor wrote to the managing editor of the *New York Evening Mail* and helped him to secure a position there.

In their parlor at 124 West 13th Street, Frank and Esther Adams placed two pianos. ◆ ◆ ◆

At age twenty-two, Adams began his "Always in Good Humor" column at the *Evening Mail*, an afternoon paper locked in a circulation war with other dailies. The column launched on October 21, 1904, and it was a hit. With his newly minted status, Adams married Minna Schwartze on his twenty-third birthday, a few weeks later. Mayor George B. McClellan presided over the City Hall ceremony. The couple's first apartment was in a brownstone at **247 West 50th Street** in Hell's Kitchen.

Soon after, Adams renamed his column "The Conning Tower" for the armored pilothouses on battleships. While other writers penned pieces about the Astors and Vanderbilts, Adams preferred to write about regular people. He sprinkled his columns with what he was doing, where he went, who beat him at tennis, and what his wife said about it. Thousands of readers knew about his home life, what he ate, what shows he saw, and even his cat.

In 1911, he began his "Diary of Our Own Samuel Pepys" column (which continued for 2.5 million words, through 1934). In 1919 he and Minna were living at **603 West 111th Street,** just west of Broadway, in Morningside Heights. In 1920 they moved around the corner to **612 West 112th Street,** up the street from the Cathedral of St. John the Divine. The next year Adams left the *Tribune* for the *World.* By then the Round Table was in full swing, and F.P.A. was the senior member.

F.P.A. divorced Minna in 1924, shocking readers who had devoured details about his personal life for almost twenty years. He took a five-month break from the column, and in Greenwich, Connecticut, on May 9, 1925, married Esther Sayles Root, a friend of Edna St. Vincent Millay's, and fifteen years younger than his first wife. The couple had three sons and a daughter. By 1928 the growing family lived at **124 West 13th Street** and later at **26 West 10th Street.** Of the former location, E. B. White said: "I used to walk quickly past the house in West 13th Street between Sixth and Seventh where F. P. A. lived, and the block seemed to tremble under my feet—the way Park Avenue trembles when a train leaves Grand Central."

## ROBERT BENCHLEY

Among the funniest writers of the twentieth century, Benchley was a study in contrasts. A straitlaced, Harvard-educated office worker, he married his college sweetheart, volunteered to help underprivileged boys, and eschewed alcohol. But something snapped after he joined the Vicious Circle in his thirties. He fell into heavy drinking, carefree spending, and young mistresses.

Robert Charles Benchley was born on September 15, 1889, in Worcester, Massachusetts. An unremarkable student, he graduated from Harvard in 1912. He and his college sweetheart, Gertrude Darling, married in June 1914 and had two sons. In 1916 he worked briefly on the *New-York Tribune* as a reporter, a job procured with the help of F.P.A. Benchley failed, though, admitting that he wasn't cut out to be a newspaperman.

Benchley transitioned from a small Broadway appearance to two decades in Hollywood comedies. ◆ ◆ ◆

He kicked around town doing small writing jobs until 1919 when Frank Crowninshield, right-hand man to publisher Condé Nast, tapped Benchley to be the first managing editor of ***Vanity Fair.*** He was working at the magazine at **19–25 West 44th Street,** alongside Parker—ultimately his closest friend—and Robert E. Sherwood, when the Round Table began. When Parker was dismissed from the magazine in January 1920, Benchley and Sherwood resigned in protest. The men joined *Life*, a weekly humor magazine, with Benchley as dramatic critic. "The theatre would be much better off if everyone, with the exception of me and a few of my friends, stayed at home," he wrote that year. "And even then I should like to go alone once in a while."

Benchley's life changed in 1922. He appeared in a revue staged by the Vicious Circle, doing a parody of a small-town community speaker. His performance of "The Treasurer's Report" brought the house down. Audience members Irving Berlin and producer Jed Harris begged him to join the Music Box Revue, an annual production of comedy, music, and dance at the **Music Box Theatre, 239 West 45th Street.** Benchley asked for $500 a week (about $6,700 today); to his total shock, the producers agreed.

Benchley became an instant celebrity, and fame followed him into the early talking pictures and, later, radio broadcasting. His first film, *The Treasurer's Report* (1928), was the first all-talking film. The Library of Congress later added his second, *The Sex Life of the Polyp* (also 1928), to the National Film Registry for preservation in perpetuity. In 1935, *How to Sleep* won the Academy Award for best short subject comedy.

Benchley's family lived in Westchester County while he rented rooms in Manhattan. He shared a room with Charles MacArthur in one of the city's first skyscrapers at the **Shelton Club Hotel, 525 Lexington Avenue** (today the New York Marriott East Side). Benchley later boarded at the Algonquin, but the nonstop party in his suite drove him across the street to the **Royalton Hotel, 44 West 44th Street,** where he lived for more than twenty years. Benchley became a victim of his own success. His writing talents landed him performing jobs that paid him large sums, but then he had no time to write, so he quit altogether.

Benchley and MacArthur lived here; today it's the Marriott East Side. ◆ ◆ ◆

## HEYWOOD BROUN

The quintessential news-paperman in a rumpled suit, Broun lived life to its fullest, never doing anything in moderation. He sported a long over-coat (sometimes of rac-coon) and a fedora with phone numbers written inside. He chain-smoked and never left home without his hip flask of gin and bitters. He loved high-stakes poker, rou-lette, and the ponies, but he also wrote beautifully and voluminously—as

Heywood Broun could write a newspaper column in less than thirty minutes. ◆ ◆ ◆

much as two thousand words a day for more than twenty years.

Broun was born at **55 Pineapple Street** in Brooklyn Heights on December 7, 1888. His father owned a successful printing and sta-tionery business. Like Dorothy Parker, he was raised on the Upper West Side, growing up in a brownstone at **140 West 87th Street.** He attended the prestigious Horace Mann School for Boys, then in Morningside Heights, where he was voted best all-around man. He also attended Harvard, but to his lifelong chagrin didn't graduate in 1910 because he couldn't pass French.

Returning from Cambridge, he took up journalism, cover-ing sports for the New York *Morning Telegraph*. Two years later he asked for a raise and was fired, at which point he joined F.P.A.

Heywood Broun took up painting as a form of stress relief. He painted only landscapes, calling each one an "Early Broun." ◆ ◆ ◆

at the *Tribune.* By age twenty-two, Broun had become a fixture at ballparks, boxing rings, and horse tracks, friendly with editors, prizefighters, and taxi drivers alike. Broun often played cards in the afternoon with Giants pitcher Christy Mathewson, and in the evening hit the town with Russian ballerina Lydia Lopokova, to whom he was engaged briefly. For the next decade he worked as a reporter, rewrite man, copyreader, Sunday magazine editor, drama critic, book reviewer, and columnist.

Broun was an iconoclast, and he married one, too: Ruth Hale, a proto-feminist. The couple had an open marriage and three activities in common: writing, fighting, and moonlighting. They were among the first to join the Vicious Circle, and they counted group members among their closest friends.

When they married in 1917, Broun was dramatic editor of the *Tribune*, but he still lived with his parents, at **195 Claremont Avenue,** in Harlem. By 1920, the couple and their young son, Heywood III, lived at **200 West 56th Street,** today the **Manhattan Club.** The following year Broun joined the *World*, and as his social consciousness increased, his genial columns became serious political discussions, drawing national attention. During the Sacco-Vanzetti trial, his views differed sharply with management, who sacked him. He ran for Congress to represent the Upper East Side as a socialist—unsuccessfully—but he attacked indignities wherever he saw them, and helped displaced workers during the Great Depression.

The brownstone owned by Broun and Hale at **333 West 85th Street,** near Riverside Park, was one of the central residences of the Round Table. Broun won the mortgage at the card table, but several years later the family had to move after he lost the deed, also while gambling. Parties at the house were raucous and legendary, and temporary lodgers here included Grant, Ross, and Taylor.

In the Thirties, Broun helped found the Newspaper Guild and traveled the country as a labor organizer, campaigning for employment reform and fair wages. He moved to a farmhouse outside Stamford, Connecticut, and his marriage to Hale ended in 1933. He married dancer Connie Madison in 1935, and Broun's name became closely linked to prominent left-wing causes of the era. Broun spent most of the Thirties as a labor organizer, and campaigned for social issues like equal employment and fair wages.

## Marc Connelly

To be a Round Table member, you had to be talented, witty, and charming. Connelly was all three, in spades. When the mood struck him, he wrote marvelous plays and short stories. Some of the greatest Vicious Circle quips came from his lips, and he was a supremely gifted raconteur, renowned in elite New York society as the ultimate dinner guest. He won the Pulitzer Prize for Drama in 1930, and coasted on that fame for fifty years.

Connelly coasted on his early fame for most of his life. He worked in theater and film for the rest of his career, but he peaked by age thirty-nine. ◆ ◆ ◆

Marcus Cook Connelly was born on December 13, 1890, in McKeesport, Pennsylvania. His father owned a boardinghouse, and young Marcus grew up among the transient hustle-bustle of a hotel. He attended a local boarding school and fell in love with the traveling theater shows that passed through nearby Pittsburgh. His family couldn't afford to send him to college, so he went to work in the advertising department of the *Pittsburgh Press*, which led to a reporter's job and a humor column when he was barely out of his teens.

He wrote one-act plays for a local community theater and was just twenty-two years old when the first was produced. His big break came when a producer took one of his shows to New York to test the waters. Connelly went along, but didn't have the train fare to return to Pittsburgh. He stayed in Manhattan with a friend and looked for a job instead.

By 1915 Connelly was selling light pieces to the *New York Sun* and the weekly humor magazine *Life*. He also wrote title cards for silent pictures in Chelsea, New York's movie hub then. The next year he moved into an apartment with seven struggling writers and artists, including illustrator John Held Jr., at **39 West 37th Street,** but had a hard time making the $2 weekly rent. Connelly avoided serving in World War I because he had to support his widowed mother. He spent the war years writing theater news for the New York *Morning Telegraph*, a paper that contained so much Broadway gossip that its nickname was "the chorus girl's breakfast." There Connelly met Broun, a drama critic for the paper.

Connelly also crossed paths with George S. Kaufman, who had the theater beat at the *Times*. In 1920 powerful producers George C. Tyler and Harry Frazee tapped Connelly and Kaufman to create a comedy vehicle for rising young English actress Lynn Fontanne. The pair turned to Algonquin pal F.P.A. for inspiration. Adams had a running character in his column, a ditzy girl named Dulcy (after Dulcinea from *Don Quixote*), who always found herself in trouble but somehow managed to save the day. Connelly and Kaufman took her as inspiration and wrote the snappy three-act *Dulcy*, which opened on Broadway in August 1921 at the **Frazee Theatre (formerly at 254 West 42nd Street**). It launched Fontanne to superstardom and ran for almost 250 performances.

# Round Table Love Triangle

Both Marc Connelly and Robert E. Sherwood married Madeline Hurlock, a silent-film star. They all remained friends. ◆ ◆ ◆

In 1930, Marc Connelly married for the first and only time. His bride, Madeline Hurlock, a beautiful former silent-film star, had appeared in more than fifty comedy shorts. The couple married in Manhattan's Municipal Building with Robert Benchley as a witness. They honeymooned in Havana, but their rocky marriage lasted only four years. She divorced him in 1935 and married his friend Robert E. Sherwood that summer in Budapest. Connelly quipped that his ex-wife was the only woman to marry two Pulitzer Prize–winning playwrights. After Connelly's divorce, his mother moved back in with him.

Connelly and Kaufman followed their success with *To The Ladies* (1922), starring a young Helen Hayes; *Merton of the Movies* (1922); the Kalmar and Ruby musical *Helen of Troy, New York* (1923); the flop, *The Deep Tangled Wildwood* (1923); the hit, *Beggar on Horseback* (1924); and another musical, *Be Yourself* (1924). They last collaborated on *The Wisdom Tooth* (1926) before parting ways.

Two years later Connelly received a copy of Roark Bradford's *Ol' Man Adam an' His Chillun*, the Old Testament retold as family stories handed down from field hands in the Old South. From it he created a legendary show and a rousing success that touched audiences and broke racial barriers in American theater. *The Green Pastures* featured the first large all-black musical cast on Broadway. Playing at the **Mansfield Theatre (now the Brooks Atkinson, 256–262 West 47th Street)**, the show ran for almost 650 performances from 1930 to 1931, and earned Connelly the Pulitzer.

Connelly had lived at **47 West 37th Street** with his mother, Mabel, in the Twenties. When his success came, they moved to **21 West 87th Street**. In 1930, when his play was the biggest hit on Broadway, they still resided together, at **152 West 57th Street.**


## EDNA FERBER

The hardest-working member of the Round Table was Edna Ferber. The *Times* claimed that for years Ferber wrote a thousand words a day, six days a week, 350 days a year. Ferber took issue with being remembered as an Algonquin habitué, though. In her autobiography, she put her attendance at about four times a year. The reason? She was always working. She wrote eight plays, twelve novels, and more than a hundred short stories. In the whole group, she was the most commercially successful.

Like many Round Tablers, her roots lay in the Midwest. She was born on August 15, 1885, in Kalamazoo, Michigan, to storekeepers, but instead of college, where the good student hoped to go, she went to work. At age seventeen, she became a reporter in Appleton, Wisconsin. Working on the *Daily Crescent* and, later, the *Milwaukee Journal* gave her the tools she used as a novelist. She developed a keen eye for detail and a knack

Winner of the Pulitzer Prize, Edna Ferber was inducted into the New York State Writers Hall of Fame in 2012. ◆ ◆ ◆

for talking to strangers, meeting traveling salesmen, store clerks, laborers, and farmers that eventually populated her fiction. She liked and wrote about ordinary men and women, and her mother provided the biggest inspiration for her work.

In her early twenties, she battled depression, returning home to convalesce. She bought a used typewriter, and shortly thereafter cranked out her first short story, "The Heroic Heroine," about an unattractive, ungainly woman, for *Everybody's Magazine*, which paid her $50 for it. She quit journalism to write more short stories, including scores featuring Emma McChesney, a traveling underwear saleswoman. Her first novel, *Dawn O'Hara, The Girl Who Laughed* (1911), tells the story of a woman newspaper reporter in Milwaukee.

Ferber lived in Chicago when she wrote her early short stories. In 1912 she moved to the **Hotel Belleclaire, 250 West 77th Street,** in New York. She often lived in residential hotels, including the **Hotel Majestic** on the corner of **72nd and Central Park West,** but a plaque commemorates her on just one of them, at **50 Central Park West**, where she lived for seven years. In 1929 she moved to the **Barbizon Hotel for Women (called Barbizon 63 today), 140 East 63rd Street.**

Ferber had her biggest success in 1924 with *So Big*, the story of a Chicagoland farmwife and her struggle with life and the soil at the turn of the century. It won the Pulitzer Prize for Fiction, was adapted into film twice, and sold more than 250,000 copies. Ferber wrote only about Americans: life on the Mississippi in *Show Boat*, the development of Oklahoma in *Cimarron*, oil-rich Texas in *Giant*, and New York in *Saratoga Trunk*.

Ferber adored Broadway and collaborated with George S. Kaufman several times before World War II. They made for a rocky team, but they made it work. Ferber and Kaufman cowrote *Minick* in 1924, based on one of her short stories, which played for five months at the Booth Theatre. They teamed up again for more hits: *The Royal Family* (1927), based on the Barrymore family, and the classics *Dinner at Eight* (1932) and *Stage Door* (1936).

Ferber never married. "Being an old maid is like death by drowning," she said. "A really delightful sensation after you cease to struggle."

## Margalo Gillmore

The Algonquin nickname of the youngest member of the Round Table was "Baby." Margalo Gillmore was just twenty-one years old when the lunches started, but she was already known to the Broadway regulars at the table. At the time, she was still living with her parents at **20 Beekman Place.** Her mother had instructed her as a teen that when she couldn't get home for lunch she should go nowhere else but the Algonquin, where the staff could look after her, and in the Twenties, Gillmore appeared regularly in shows just a few minutes' walk from the hotel.

Margalo Gillmore in Eugene O'Neill's *The Straw* (1921). ◆ ◆ ◆

Gillmore was a third-generation actor; her parents and grandparents had spent many years on stages in England and America. Her parents, American actors Frank Gillmore and Laura MacGillivray, were on tour in England when Margalo was born on May 31, 1897, in London. The family returned to America two years later, and she grew up in a fourth-floor walk-up at **615 West 136th Street.** As a child, all she ever thought about was performing: "I learned from it never to be late; when I walked to school I pretended I was on my way to a rehearsal. When I learned to read, I conquered the dull drudgery only because someday I might have a part in a play. At night in my bed I dreamed of my dressing room I might have one day."

The childhood home of actress sisters Margalo and Ruth Gillmore, 615 West 136th Street. ◆ ◆ ◆

Her father helped to found the Actors' Equity Association, and she was among the first union members to get a card. She made her Broadway debut in September 1917 in *The Scrap of Paper*, a three-act comedy based on stories from the *Saturday Evening Post*, at the **Criterion Theatre, 1514 Broadway.** Her first leading role came two years later in *The Famous Mrs. Fair* at **Henry Miller's Theatre, 124 West 43rd Street.** The drama took place in New York and Long Island and ran for nearly two hundred performances. Gillmore's star rose in 1922 when she starred in *He Who Gets Slapped* at the **Garrick Theatre, 67 West 35th Street.** One reviewer called Gillmore "the most interesting and the most promising young actress on the American stage."

In 1935, approaching forty, she married Robert Ross, a Canadian actor-director five years her junior at her parents' apartment at **31 Beekman Place.** She and Ross played husband and wife onstage

in 1953 in the hit *Kind Sir*, until he died in February the following year. Also in 1954 she played Mrs. Darling in *Peter Pan*, alongside Mary Martin, at the **Winter Garden Theatre, 1634 Broadway.**
CBS telecast the show live to an audience of sixty-five million view-
ers. She performed the role of Mrs. Van Daan in the theatrical adaptation of *The Diary of Anne Frank*, which ran from 1955 to 1957.
Altogether, she made more than twenty-five motion picture and
television appearances, but her most memorable role onscreen was
as Grace Kelly's mother in *High Society*, in 1956.


## Jane Grant

Among her many gifts, Jane Grant had a beautiful singing voice and
a head for business. Her vocal talents landed her a one-way ticket
from Kansas to Manhattan, but her savvy writing and business skills
made a lasting mark and gave readers one of the greatest magazines
ever. She was the driving force behind the birth of *The New Yorker*,
pushing her first husband, Harold Ross, to realize their dream of
starting a magazine. "There would be no *New Yorker* today if it were
not for her," Ross said in 1945. "He would have given up, I am sure, if
I hadn't encouraged him," Grant said after Ross's death. "Fortunately
I was able to influence him, for he was in love with me."

Although she came from humble Midwest stock, Jeannette Cole
Grant was destined to rub shoulders with the Manhattan elite. She
was born on May 29, 1892, in Joplin, Missouri, to a farmer father
and teacher mother. Her mother died when she was six, and the
family moved to Girard, Kansas, to be close to her maternal relatives.
She was a good student with a talent for singing, but young women
in Girard at the time had only two paths in life: farmwife or school-
teacher. Young Jeanette wanted neither.

Jane Grant and Harold Ross, three years before they launched *The New Yorker*, outside their Hell's Kitchen home at 412 West 47th Street. Over the decades Grant has been left out of the history of the magazine's creation; however, Ross admitted that without her *The New Yorker* would never have gotten off the ground. ◆ ◆ ◆

She talked her family into allowing her to go to New York to take voice lessons for a year after she graduated from high school, after which she would return to Kansas to take up a teaching post. She had never been farther east than Kansas City when she took the 1,300-mile railroad journey to New York in 1908. She was just sixteen years old and lived in Roselle Park, New Jersey, a 25-mile train ride to Manhattan.

A couple of years later she moved into the **Three Arts Club**—a residence for young women studying drama, music, and fine art—at **340 West 85th Street.** Several high-society women at the club took an interest in the girls and tried to plane their rough edges. One of them helped the farmer's daughter transform herself into a smooth conversationalist and charming dinner guest. When her singing career didn't take off, Grant enrolled in business school. In 1912 she took a clerical job at *Collier's Weekly.* Two years later she landed a job at the *Times* answering phones in the society department for $10 a week. The paper's legendary managing editor, Carl Van Anda, told her that while women were tolerated on the staff, there was no chance for advancement.

A newsroom darling, she taught the men to dance, and they taught her to gamble and curse. While there, Grant befriended a young Alexander Woollcott, a city-room reporter at the time. By 1915 she was covering events and writing her own stories for the paper, crossing from society department to city desk and becoming the first female general assignment reporter on the *New York Times.* Soon she was bouncing around town, from operas with Enrico Caruso to ballgames at the Polo Grounds. At the time, she lived in a rented room at **119 West 47th Street,** not far from her future home with Ross, and then later, across the street from Carnegie Hall.

When America entered the war, she begged to be sent as a correspondent. The paper refused her request. Seeing Woollcott

Jane Grant talked her way into the YMCA to go to France. ◆ ◆ ◆

volunteer and enlist in a hospital company doubled her determination, so she joined the YMCA, which was sending women over to help the troops by singing, setting up dances, and screening movies. She arrived in late 1918, earning $108 a month—more than the *Times* was paying her.

In France, Grant met many future Round Tablers. Woollcott introduced her to his *Stars and Stripes* editor, Harold Ross. The two dated briefly in Paris, but Grant had other suitors, and kept him at bay until the war ended. When she returned to New York in the summer of 1919, the *Times* promoted her to editor of hotel news. Ross and Grant married the next year, and briefly lived in the Algonquin Hotel. The couple rented a bedroom in the home of Broun and Hale for a summer. A year later, with close friend Ruth Hale, Grant cofounded the Lucy Stone League, a forerunner of the Women's Liberation Movement. Its motto was: "My name is the symbol for my identity and must not be lost." Maintaining her maiden name was a lifelong crusade.

In 1922 Ross and Grant bought an apartment building at **412 West 47th Street.** Soon after, she pushed him to get their magazine idea off the ground. She helped pitch the proposal to investors and talked it up to her wide circle of friends and associates. Grant landed Ross an appointment with investor Raoul Fleischmann, who bankrolled the magazine. Grant should also take credit for launching Janet Flanner's career. She met Flanner through Neysa McMein and showed Ross letters that Flanner wrote from Paris, urging him to hire her to write for the magazine. He did, calling her Genêt, which he thought was Janet in French. Flanner wrote her "Letter from Paris" for fifty years, earning her the US National Book Award.

When Grant's marriage to Ross fell apart just three years after the magazine launched, she didn't seek alimony. Instead, she wanted fair compensation for the hard work she had put into making the magazine a success. Ross agreed to $10,000 a year, to come from his own stock dividends. For the next twenty years, Grant chased down checks from her ex-husband.

After the divorce, Grant traveled the world and wrote freelance pieces. She became the first female *Times* reporter in China and Russia in the early Thirties, interviewing political leaders and the ordinary people she met, but neither the *Times* nor *The New Yorker* has ever paid proper tribute to her pioneering achievements.

Grant's second marriage was to William B. Harris, an editor on *Fortune*, in June 1939. The couple bought land in Litchfield, Connecticut, named it White Flower Farm, and Grant began an entirely new chapter of her life.

## Ruth Hale

James Abbe took this portrait of Ruth Hale when she was thirty-six. ◆ ◆ ◆

There was no bigger iconoclast sitting at the Round Table than Ruth Hale. The writer-publicist was married to Heywood Broun, but nobody dared call her Mrs. Broun. Hale was a writer, editor, and publicist, but she was most famous for her "fanatical" devotion to women's rights in the Jazz Age. Hale was the driving force behind the Lucy Stone League, a group that supported married women keeping their maiden names legally.

Hale was Southern by birth, but she didn't fit the stereotype of easygoing grace, charm, and humility. In fact, she took great pride in losing her Southern accent.

She was born in Rogersville, Tennessee, on July 5, 1886. Her father was an attorney and her mother, a high school mathematics teacher. When she was ten, her father died, and three years later Hale was sent to boarding school at the Hollins Institute (today, Hollins University) in Roanoke, Virginia. At age sixteen, she enrolled in the Drexel Academy of Fine Art (today Drexel University) in Philadelphia, with dreams of becoming an artist.

When Hale was eighteen years old she became a journalist in Washington, D.C., writing for the Hearst syndicate. She worked at the *Washington Post* briefly before returning in her twenties to Pennsylvania and the drama department of the *Philadelphia Public Ledger*. Hale also tried sportswriting decades before other women took it up.

Around 1915 Hale moved to New York and sold small pieces to the *Times*, the *Tribune*, and Condé Nast magazines. She took bit parts on Broadway and posed for artistic nude portraits for fashion photographer Nickolas Muray. She became a sought-after theatrical publicist and worked for the top producers.

Alice Duer Miller introduced Hale to Broun at a New York Giants baseball game at the Polo Grounds. They married in 1917. Hale begrudgingly accepted a traditional church wedding but refused to walk down the aisle until the organist ceased playing Mendelssohn's "Wedding March." When the war started, the newlyweds went to France as correspondents. After several months in Paris, Hale became pregnant. Returning to New York, the couple set up house at **333 West 85th Street.** The unusual marriage had Hale on the first floor and Broun occupying the second.

In 1918 Hale gave birth to the couple's only child, Heywood "Woodie" Broun III. (As an adult, Woodie took his mother's name, and was known as sportscaster Heywood Hale Broun.) The couple led completely separate lives.

In 1921 she took a stand with the US State Department, demanding that she be issued a passport as Ruth Hale, not Mrs. Heywood Broun. The government refused; up until that time, no woman had ever been given a passport with her maiden name. She was unable to cut through the red tape, and the government issued her passport reading "Ruth Hale, also known as Mrs. Heywood

Broun." She refused to accept the passport and canceled her trip to France. So did her husband.

In May 1921 she was issued a New York City real estate deed in her own name—believed to be the first ever given to a married woman—for an apartment house on Manhattan's Upper West Side. Not long afterward, she was chosen president of the Lucy Stone League. Her husband was among the men present; other Lucy Stoners were F.P.A. and his second wife, Esther Root; Janet Flanner; Jane Grant; Beatrice Kaufman; and John Barrymore's playwright wife, Michael Strange (Blanche Oelrichs). Hale made headlines in August 1927 when she took a leading role in protesting the executions of accused anarchists Sacco and Vanzetti, traveling to Boston for the unsuccessful defense committee.

In the Twenties, she worked as a theatrical press agent, reviewed books for the *Brooklyn Daily Eagle*, and ghost-wrote many of Broun's columns. In 1925 she became one of the earliest contributors to *The New Yorker*'s "Talk of the Town." About the time the Round Table ran out of steam, so did Hale. She moved out of New York to a ramshackle farmhouse, called Sabine Farm, in Stamford, Connecticut.

As the Twenties ended, Hale spent considerable time fighting for women's rights and less time in journalism. Hale and Broun were quietly divorced in Nogales, Mexico, in November 1933.


## BEATRICE KAUFMAN

The Vicious Circle rarely tolerated wives. Alexander Woollcott, de facto ruler of the table, allowed Beatrice Kaufman to attend partly because of his loyalty to her husband, George. But Beatrice knew she couldn't remain an unemployed woman in their midst, nor did she live in the shadow of her famous playwright husband. She carved out her own identity, working in Broadway publicity, and later taking a

One of the most beloved women in the group was Beatrice Kaufman. ◆ ◆ ◆

job as a reader for publisher Horace Liveright.

Beatrice Bakrow was born on January 20, 1895, in Rochester, New York, to middle-class parents in the textile business. She was tall, heavy, and not very attractive, but she made up for it by being funny, charming, stylish, and a good conversationalist. She studied briefly at Wellesley, but was kicked out freshman year for breaking curfew.

In the summer of 1916, during a party for her cousin Allan Friedlich and his new wife, Ruth Kaufman, she met the bride's younger brother, George, a backup drama critic on the *New York Times* making $36 a week. Shy, quiet, and withdrawn, the reporter hit it off with the funny girl; she talked, and he listened. The two couples visited Niagara Falls together, and the next day Beatrice announced to her family that she and George were getting married.

They wed in March 1917 in Rochester, with F.P.A. as best man and no money for a honeymoon. The couple had an unusual twenty-eight-year marriage. Not long after their wedding, Beatrice miscarried. It devastated the couple, but George took it to another level. He couldn't bear to have a sexual relationship with his wife, and never did again. From then on, they had an open marriage while maintaining the outward appearance of a normally married couple. When George found himself in a national sex scandal with actress

Mary Astor in 1936, Beatrice stood by him even as the press chased her husband across the country. For his part, he always had her read his plays before anyone else.

In the span of a few years she reinvented herself as a society woman, appearing in gossip columns for hosting charity events and gala parties. When the Round Table began, the couple lived at **241 West 101st Street.** By 1920 they had relocated a mile south, to **150 West 80th Street.** Five years later they rented an apartment at

Her husband's tawdry 1936 sex scandal forced Beatrice Kaufman into the spotlight. ◆ ◆ ◆

**200 West 58th Street.** They also lived for a time in the Hotel Majestic, on the corner of West 72nd Street and Central Park West. In 1934, when her husband was among the best-paid men on Broadway, the Kaufmans lived at **14 East 94th Street.**

One of Bea Kaufman's closest friends on the Round Table was Margaret "Peggy" Leech. In 1934 the pair went to Jamaica to work up a play they hoped to stage. Their only Broadway show, *Divided by Three*, tells the story of a middle-aged woman who falls in love with another man but who won't leave her husband. The play opened in the Ethel Barrymore Theatre but received tepid reviews, despite starring Judith Anderson and Hedda Hopper. It also had the poor luck to open the same week as a play penned by her husband and Moss Hart, *Merrily We Roll Along*, a much bigger hit. *Divided by Three* only lasted a month.

In February 1936, Carmel Snow hired Beatrice as the *Harper's Bazaar* fiction editor. Later that year, Samuel Goldwyn contracted for her services as a script reader and story editor for his movie studio. As World War II began, the Kaufmans were wealthy celebrities worthy of a splashy pictorial in *Life* with Moss Hart and Harpo Marx.

## GEORGE S. KAUFMAN

At every stage of George S. Kaufman's career was a member of the Round Table. Frank Adams gave the Pittsburgh native his first break by including him in "The Conning Tower" and securing a job for him at the *Tribune*. He wrote his first hit show, *Dulcy*, with Marc Connelly, and also collaborated with Aleck Woollcott, Edna Ferber, and Ring Lardner. Kaufman stayed active as a playwright, editor, producer, director, and actor

George S. Kaufman influenced playwrights such as Woody Allen, Mel Brooks, and Neil Simon. ◆ ◆ ◆

in New York for more than forty years. He wrote or cowrote forty-five plays (more than half of them hits). He and Morrie Ryskind won the 1932 Pulitzer for *Of Thee I Sing*, and Kaufman won the 1937 prize with Moss Hart for *You Can't Take It with You*.

Kaufman was born in Pittsburgh, Pennsylvania, on November 14, 1889. He wasn't given a middle name at birth. To mimic Franklin P. Adams, who also had adopted a middle initial, Kaufman chose

"S" so that he too would have three letters in "The Conning Tower," as G.S.K. (later, he claimed, for Simon). Kaufman married Beatrice Bakrow in 1917. They adopted a daughter, Anne, in 1925, and lived at **158 West 58th Street** before moving to **14 East 94th Street.**

On their fifth wedding anniversary, Woollcott sent a telegram to the Kaufmans: I HAVE BEEN LOOKING AROUND FOR AN APPROPRIATE WOODEN GIFT AND AM PLEASED HEREBY TO PRESENT YOU WITH ELSIE FERGUSON'S PERFORMANCE IN HER NEW PLAY.

Kaufman once slipped out of a theater during the performance of one of his shows to send a telegram to an actor in the cast that read: I AM WATCHING YOUR PERFORMANCE FROM THE LAST ROW. WISH YOU WERE HERE. His comebacks were equally legendary. An actress told him that she had trained her dog to curl himself around her neck and remain motionless while she entered hotel lobbies, as a sort of living fur neckpiece. "I taught my dog the trick for a special reason," she told Kaufman. "Hotels are silly enough to keep dogs out entirely. Now that my Fido can look so much like a fur piece, I can smuggle him into all the hotels on earth."

"And how do you get in yourself?" he asked.

In public, Kaufman avoided off-color humor, but in private he and his wife had an open marriage that allowed for discreet indiscretions and, in George's case, a charge account at Polly Adler's brothel. In the summer of 1936, Kaufman's name hit front pages from coast to coast. Actress Mary Astor was embroiled in a child custody case with her husband, and her diary was leaked to the press. "We saw every show in town," she wrote. "Had grand fun together and went frequently to 73rd Street where he fucked the living daylights out of me." A court subpoena sent Kaufman to hide out at Moss Hart's house. Even afterward, Kaufman was astonished to see himself portrayed as a sexual dynamo:

I can't understand why there should have been so much public interest in the case. The public doesn't care about writers. Miss Astor is no longer a big figure in pictures. I just can't understand it. . . . There is one thing I resent about the case. Some newspapermen referred to me as a middle-aged playwright. I am middle-aged. That's why I didn't like it, I suspect.

Four years after Beatrice died, Kaufman married Leueen Mac-Grath, a ravishing blonde English actress twenty-five years his junior. Kaufman was her third husband, and they lived at **410 Park Avenue.**

## Margaret Leech

Of the five members of the Round Table to win a Pulitzer Prize, Margaret Leech received the honor twice. She was one of the least known of the famous group, but among its members she was the most loyal friend.

Born on November 7, 1893, in Newburgh, New York, Leech graduated from Vassar in 1915 before gravitating toward a writing career that began with Condé Nast's magazines. In 1920 she lived at **315 West 79th Street** with her parents,

Margaret Leech wrote short stories and novels before becoming a dedicated presidential historian. ◆ ◆ ◆

and later at **315 West 97th Street.** Leech wrote a handful of articles for *The New Yorker,* including several profiles of women newsmakers.

In the Twenties, Peggy Leech rented an apartment at 36 West 12th Street, near Washington Square Park. ◆ ◆ ◆

She dabbled in stage acting but never pursued it seriously. Her nickname at the Vicious Circle was "Peaches and Cream" for her wholesome good looks and demeanor.

In her thirties she wrote two novels, *The Back of the Book* (1924) and *Tin Wedding* (1926), both receiving strong reviews. At the time she was living at **36 West 12th Street.** In 1927 she collaborated with Heywood Broun on a biography of postal inspector Anthony Comstock, who in 1873 had founded the infamous New York Society for the Suppression of Vice. Written in the era of enforced censorship and speakeasy raids, *Anthony Comstock: Roundsman of the Lord*'s subject matter seemed eerily relevant once again. It was Leech's first book of nonfiction. Broun and Leech wrote alternating chapters, but their partnership had its challenges: One story has it that when Leech went to Broun's house to pick up the manuscript, he couldn't find it in his messy room. Nevertheless, the book was a critical and commercial success, and the first Book of the Month pick.

In 1928 she wrote her last novel, *The Feathered Nest*, before turning entirely to nonfiction. She also worked as a correspondent for the *World*. The next year, *Harper's* published her short story "Manicure," a tale of adultery that became a sensation and found a place in *The Best Stories of 1929*, a collection that also included Willa Cather.

In August 1928, Leech married Ralph Pulitzer—eldest son of publisher Joseph, president and editor of the *World*, and a divorcé with two grown sons—at the **Community Church of New York, 40 East 35th Street.** Reverend John H. Holmes, one of the most famous religious leaders in the nation, officiated at the ceremony. They resided first at **450 East 52nd Street** (with eight servants) before moving to their permanent home at **120 East End Avenue.** The couple had two daughters: Margaretta, who died at the age of sixteen months while the couple was vacationing in St.-Jean-de-Luz, France, and Susan, born in 1932.

Ralph Pulitzer suffered the enmity of many journalists for closing and selling the *World* in 1931. He and his wife traveled the world so he could pursue big-game hunting in Central America, West Africa, and India. He died following abdominal surgery on June 14, 1939; she never remarried.

After the death of her husband, Leech devoted herself to writing full-time. She commuted from New York to Washington for five years to work on *Reveille in Washington: 1860–1865*, earning the ire of the War Department by asking to see files on spies arrested during the Civil War. When the government refused to grant her access, she said: "What do you think I might do with the Secret Service reports of 1862? Sell them to the Japanese?" Published in 1941, the book won the Pulitzer for history and earned her such regard that Newburgh offered to hold a Margaret Leech Day. "I shall ride back and forth under the triumphal arch all afternoon, if they have a triumphal arch," she joked. Some questioned the fairness of an author winning a prize named for her father-in-law, but *Time* magazine praised the book's fine writing and proclaimed that she had earned the award "with no hint of nepotism." Civil War historians still consider it a classic text.

Eighteen years later, she won her second Pulitzer for *In the Days of William McKinley*, published in 1959. She was the first woman to win the prize for history, and she remains the only woman to have won it twice. *In the Days of McKinley* also earned her a National Book Award and Columbia University's Bancroft Prize in American History. As a widow raising her surviving daughter, Susan, Leech lived in Gracie Square and in Lenox, Massachusetts, the cultural heart of the Berkshires. Leech told an interviewer that her apartment had two bathtubs: one for bathing, the other to store her notebooks while writing. Her closest friends within the Vicious Circle were Ferber and McMein.

## NEYSA McMEIN

Marc Connelly fondly recalled Neysa McMein as the woman who "rode elephants in circus parades and dashed from her studio to follow passing fire engines." She held sway over the group, which was drawn

In today's money, McMein earned about a quarter of a million dollars annually for her cover illustrations. She was also in demand for advertising campaigns for beauty, healthcare, and luxury products. ◆ ◆ ◆

to her larger-than-life personality and charisma. For twenty years, she was the most famous female artist in the country. Her distinctive, colorful covers helped sell millions of magazines. In 1929 she was called "the highest-paid woman artist in the United States."

Marjorie Moran McMein was born on January 25, 1888, in Quincy, Illinois, and after attaining fame she returned there as a celebrity but once. She studied at the Chicago Institute, and broke into advertising in her early twenties by drawing shoes and hats in the Second City. She knew that New York would be a better market for her, however, so in 1912 she moved east. When she arrived at the train station, her new name was Neysa.

She set up a studio in a commercial building at **57 West 57th Street.** Wearing pearls and a paint-smeared smock, the professional artist with a zest for life painted beautiful models for magazines that included *McCall's* and the *Saturday Evening Post*, and

McMein's painting studio became a salon for the Round Table. She could paint in the midst of cocktail parties. ◆ ◆ ◆

for ads by companies that included Palmolive and Wrigley's. While the model (sometimes a showgirl spotted on the sidewalk) posed, a party went on around them in the studio. The Algonquin crowd gravitated to McMein's after their luncheons. A visitor might see Harpo Marx clowning for Alexander Woollcott and Charles MacArthur. Cole Porter sang to Neysa while she worked; George Gershwin pounded McMein's piano. Dorothy Parker and her first husband, Edwin Pond Parker II, lived across the hall. Tallulah Bankhead, Marc Connelly, and Ruth Gordon stopped by. In 1924, Edna Ferber fashioned McMein into Dallas O'Mara in the Pulitzer Prize–winning novel, *So Big*.

Before radio and television, McMein could announce who she believed were the most beautiful women in the country, and it made headlines. She wrote magazine articles about beauty and fashion, and later a syndicated newspaper column devoted to her other passions, numerology and party games. She also teamed up with Parker: McMein would paint a portrait of a president or a prizefighter, and Parker would write an account of the sitting.

McMein lived in a brownstone at **136 West 65th Street** in 1918; the building was demolished about forty years later to make way for Lincoln Center. In 1920 she lived half a block from Madison Square Park, at **226 Fifth Avenue.**

In June 1923 she secretly married John Baragawanath, a mining engineer, but business kept him from going on their honeymoon to Europe. McMein informed Woollcott, whose response was to sail with her on the *Olympic*; Marc Connelly and violinist Jascha Heifetz tagged along. The press reported that McMein was on her honeymoon in France with three men, none of them her husband.

In December 1924, her only child, Joan, was born. The family moved to **29 East 64th Street,** where the couple hosted the wedding of Arthur Samuels and actress Vivian Martin in February 1926. McMein and her family later moved to a duplex at **131 East 66th Street,** her last address.

## HERMAN MANKIEWICZ

Mankiewicz worked for newspapers and magazines before going to Hollywood and writing *Citizen Kane.* ◆ ◆ ◆

Without Herman Jacob Mankiewicz we wouldn't have *Citizen Kane* or *Animal Crackers*. He had a career like nobody else in the Vicious Circle. As a press agent, he worked with heavyweight champ Jack Dempsey. At the *New York Times*, he worked under George S. Kaufman. When Harold Ross launched *The New Yorker*, he tapped "Mank" as a critic. When the Marx Brothers wanted to make movies, he produced them. But it was Mankiewicz's experiences in New York City and Hollywood in the Twenties that inspired him to write his masterpiece, winning the Academy Award for the screenplay of *Citizen Kane* in 1941 with Orson Welles.

A native New Yorker, Mankiewicz was born on November 7, 1897. His father was a teacher and his mother a dressmaker, both German immigrants. When Mankiewicz was a boy the family moved to Wilkes-Barre, Pennsylvania, where he grew up. He transferred his boyhood to the screen in *Citizen Kane*; the famous "Rosebud" was actually his stolen childhood bicycle. Mankiewicz was a brilliant student, admitted to Columbia when he was just fifteen years old. He earned his philosophy degree in three years and then attended graduate school. At the time he lived in the East Village at **44 St. Mark's Place.**

When World War I broke out, Mankiewicz enlisted in the US Marine Corps and shipped out to France, where his fluent German served him well. After the war, he married his sweetheart, Sara Aaronson, in Washington, D.C. The couple returned to postwar Berlin, where Mankiewicz worked for the Red Cross and, later, as a correspondent for the *Chicago Tribune*. He didn't come to New York until 1922, when the Vicious Circle was already an institution. Mankiewicz went to work at the *World*, where he met Broun and F.P.A. A year later, he moved to the *Times*.

Kaufman took Mankiewicz to the Algonquin for the first time. He passed the test and was allowed to come to the table whenever he liked, usually once a week. Although Mankiewicz wasn't a member of the original group, he quickly fit in. Woollcott called him "the funniest man in New York." Sherwood said he was "the truest wit of all," and Pemberton considered him "the one real wit" at the table. Mank reveled in the Vicious Circle: He drank with Dorothy Parker and Ring Lardner; F.P.A. was his poker buddy; and Harold Ross leaned on him. At lunch one afternoon, Mankiewicz turned serious and announced to the group, "I have a new baby boy, born today. His name is Frank." To which Marc Connelly replied, "Does Sara know?"

In 1926, as the Round Table was winding down, Mankiewicz went to Hollywood to pursue screenwriting. He ultimately worked on more than seventy films, both silent and talkies. From 1931 to 1933 he worked as a producer on three Marx Brothers films in a row: *Monkey Business*, *Horse Feathers*, and *Duck Soup*. He bounced from studio to studio, but as the Thirties drew to a close the planets aligned and Mankiewicz found himself working with Orson Welles. After one of his numerous crack-ups, Mankiewicz was laid up at home on bed rest. Welles visited the screenwriter daily, and *Citizen Kane*, based on Mankiewicz's childhood in Pennsylvania and journalism career in New York, took shape. The film today is remembered as Welles's masterpiece, but without Mankiewicz as the dream catcher, it wouldn't exist. Unfortunately, winning an Academy Award didn't help Mankiewicz's career, and he spent the next twenty years battling alcohol and gambling addictions.

## Harpo Marx

As a member of the Marx Brothers, Harpo Marx said nothing, and in doing so he often said more than the rest. Wearing a large, fuzzy wig—blond, pink, or scarlet by various accounts—with a moon face, large wide eyes, and a raincoat flapping open, Harpo was unforgettable. He made rapid gestures, wild expressions, and chased girls with his automobile horn. He taught himself to play his trademark harp by ear.

Harpo (Arthur), Gummo (Milton), Chico (Leonard), and in front, Groucho (Julius) Marx, about 1924. ◆ ◆ ◆

Marx wasn't an original member of the Round Table. He and his brothers had broken into the upper echelons of vaudeville in the years following World War I, and in 1924 they made their Broadway debut in *I'll Say She Is* at the **Casino Theatre, formerly at 1404 Broadway.** Woollcott stumbled upon the revue and was thunderstruck, telling his friends and readers that the Marx Brothers were in a hit. Woollcott called Harpo "the funniest man I have ever seen on the stage."

Adolph (later Arthur) Marx was born on November 23, 1888, in a tenement apartment in Yorkville to an Alsatian tailor. His mother, Minnie, was a singer. At P.S. 86, he made it as far as the second grade. Their mother pushed him and brothers Julius (Groucho), Leonard (Chico), Milton (Gummo), and Herbert (Zeppo) into saloons and dirty theaters from Coney Island to Manhattan as they developed their act. With their mother rounding out the group, they were known as the Six Musical Mascots; later they performed as the Three Nightingales, then Four. The brothers took their act on the vaudeville circuit for close to a decade before becoming famous.

On the road in Illinois in May 1914, the four brothers gathered around a poker table with vaudeville comedian Art Fisher, who gave them the names by which we know them. They sat down as Leonard, Arthur, Julius, and Milton, and stood up as Chico, Harpo, Groucho, and Gummo: Chico, because he chased girls, or chicks (the correct way to pronounce his nickname); Harpo, for his instrument; Groucho, because he always carried his grouch bag around his neck to collect tips; and Gummo, because he wore gum-soled shoes as the team's dancer.

Harpo lived with ten family members in a small apartment at **179 East 93rd Street.** By 1918, the same year the brothers played The Palace, he was living down the road at **15 East 93rd Street,** near Central Park.

At the Algonquin, Harpo was able to drop his act.

The Marx Brothers grew up in the German-Jewish section of the Upper East Side. Today a nearby playground is named in their honor. ◆ ◆ ◆

An immediate fan, Broun saw the Marx Brothers more than thirty times, worrying that his obituary would say that moving scenery in a Marx Brothers show had killed him. But the best acquaintance Harpo made at the Table was George S. Kaufman, who convinced the brothers to let him script a show. He eventually wrote *Animal Crackers* and *A Night at the Opera*.

In September 1936, Harpo married Susan Fleming, a former *Follies* dancer—nickname: "The Million-Dollar Legs"—from Forest Hills, Queens. They adopted four children.

Harpo was a blithe spirit. At dinner one night, seated next to Kaufman, the playwright noticed that Harpo's watch erroneously read 12:20. "I haven't wound it in three years," Harpo said with a smile. "It doesn't matter to me what time it is."

In 2003, the New York Parks Department named a **neighborhood playground at Second Avenue and East 96th Street** in honor of the Marx Brothers.

Actress Ilka Chase and husband William B. Murray at the Waldorf Astoria New York, 1941. ◆ ◆ ◆

## WILLIAM B. MURRAY

The cipher at the Round Table and the person who has fallen deepest into the cracks of the group's shared history is William B. Murray. He isn't remembered for anything today, although he was the one who sent out Pemberton's invitations to the first lunch, according to Margaret Case, and Murray's first wife had a forty-year romance with Janet Flanner of *The New Yorker*.

Murray was born in Scranton, Pennsylvania, on December 9, 1889, raised in Brooklyn, and graduated from Cornell. He worked as music critic for the *Brooklyn Daily Eagle* from 1918 to 1923, meeting Alexander Woollcott at the theaters and becoming friendly with publicists John Peter Toohey and Murdock Pemberton. He loved playing the chimes at Trinity Church on Wall Street. He was so popular that in 1921, Edison Records released a recording of him performing "Joy to the World" and "Hark! The Herald Angels Sing." That year he was living at **38 West 40th Street.**

In the Twenties, Murray switched from journalism to publicity, marketing grand pianos for the Baldwin Piano Company. In his role as concert manager he traveled to Europe, seeking concert artists to perform back in the States. In the summer of 1922, while in Rome on business, he met Natalia Danesi, a raven-haired Italian opera singer. The following year she came to New York, and in 1924 the couple married at Trinity Church, with Woollcott as best man. The couple had a rocky relationship and one son, William Jr., born in 1926. Danesi promptly took the boy back to Italy.

In December 1928, on the recommendation of Prime Minister Benito Mussolini, King Victor Emmanuel III awarded the Chevalier's Cross of the Order of the Crown of Italy to Murray, whose sole qualification appears to be that he married an Italian.

In September 1934, Danesi sued for divorce, granted later that year. Murray married actress Ilka Chase, a divorcée fifteen years his junior, the following year. They moved to **333 East 57th Street,** and their marriage lasted eleven years. After World War II Murray married an interior decorator, Florence Smolen, with whom he had twin boys.

As the city's premier talent agent, he rose to become the head of the radio department of the powerful **William Morris Agency (office at 1270 Sixth Avenue).** His clients included Fred Allen, Fanny Brice, Eddie Cantor, Al Jolson, and Groucho Marx. As head of the department, he created advertiser-supported shows for Abbott and Costello, Burns and Allen, and Amos and Andy, among others. One of his last projects was with client Milton Berle; in 1948 the comedian's *Texaco Star Theatre* was among the first hit TV series when the medium was born.

## DOROTHY PARKER

The poster girl for the Round Table has always been Dorothy Parker, a distinction she loathed for the rest of her life.

Born August 22, 1893, in West End, New Jersey, at her parents' summer beach cottage, Dorothy Rothschild grew up on the Upper West Side of Manhattan. Her mother died just before her fifth birthday, followed by her stepmother, before she turned ten.

Dottie rhymed sentences at a young age. In 1906, during a summer vacation in Bellport, on Long Island, she sent a postcard to her father and the family dog:

Dorothy Parker—painted here by Neysa McMein—joined *Vogue* at age twenty-one, launching her career. ◆ ◆ ◆

Dear Papa,
We are all well,
the same to you.
My love to Rags,
and now I'm through.
*Dorothy*

The aspiring poet was twenty years old when her father died at their home, **310 West 80th Street.** She spent the next year working odd jobs and writing verse. The first person to notice her talent was Frank Crowninshield, editor of *Vanity Fair.* He accepted her first piece of light verse, "Any Porch," for the September 1915 issue, for $5. Emboldened by its acceptance, she marched down to the company's offices at **19–25 West 44th Street** and asked for a job. She ultimately landed work for the company's sister publication, *Vogue*, under Edna Woolman Chase, who recalled:

> In 1915 a small, dark-haired pixie, treacle-sweet of tongue but vinegar-witted, joined our staff. Her name was Dorothy Rothschild, and she was engaged to do captions and special features. She wrote a piece about houses called "Interior Desecration," and more than one decorator swallowed hard and counted ten before expressing his feelings about it. Showing rare courage, she risked her head in the line of duty and turned in her experience under the title "Life on a Permanent Wave" when the wave was still a hazard and its most permanent aspect was the entire day required to accomplish it.

In 1917 Dorothy married Edwin Pond Parker II, a stockbroker. He enlisted in the army ambulance corps and soon was bound for France. Meanwhile, Parker migrated to *Vanity Fair*, taking up the drama critic job vacated by P. G. Wodehouse. In her legendary columns, she lambasted casts and audiences alike with vim and vigor, and she had no qualms about stepping on the toes of the powerful. It was hard to miss *Vanity Fair's* representative on Broadway.

When the Round Table began in 1919, Parker was already friendly with many of the group's members. She knew Broun through her older sister, Helen. Frank Adams ran many of her poems in his column. Woollcott was a friend from Broadway first nights. Robert Benchley and Robert E. Sherwood were coworkers. The next year, following her split from her husband, she lived alone at **235 West 71st Street.** Donald Ogden Stewart met Parker at this time at the

*Life* magazine office: "Dorothy was sort of a roving imp-at-large. She was absolutely devastating: petite, graceful, black bobbed hair, keen startling eyes."

During the Round Table's reign, Parker's legend grew to enormous proportions. Newspapers ran her words on a constant basis, and she was quoted across the country. Cole Porter even wrote her into a hit song. With her fame spreading, she became a personality. But she also had become a gifted short-story writer. She contributed some of the first short stories to *The New Yorker* in its formative years, including the classics "Arrangement in Black and White" and "Dusk before Fireworks." In 1929 the semiautobiographical "Big Blonde" won the O. Henry award for best story.

In the Thirties, she took up screenwriting, which she hated, and left-wing causes, which she loved. She and her second husband, Alan Campbell, became a hot screenwriting partnership in 1934, the year of their first marriage. In Hollywood, Parker jumped into the political scene with numerous causes, benefits, and campaigns. Her activities drew the attention of the FBI, which created a 300-page dossier on her. During World War II, she shuttled between rented mansions in Beverly Hills and a country house in Bucks County, Pennsylvania. A reporter once asked Parker to describe her house in two words. "Want it?" was her reply.

Parker spent the Forties and Fifties writing short stories for magazines, the occasional screenplay, and giving a lot of her time to political causes. In 1946 she and Campbell split, and Parker spent a few years with a young writer, Ross Evans. When that relationship ended, she and Campbell remarried in 1950. They had just enough screenwriting jobs to scrape by in West Hollywood in the Fifties, but when times were bleak the couple went to the state unemployment office together.

A few minutes after this photo was taken, Dorothy Parker was arrested outside the Massachusetts Statehouse for protesting the planned execution of anarchists Sacco and Vanzetti. ◆ ◆ ◆

# When the Algonquin Sued Dorothy Parker

Following the opening night of Philip Barry's play *Here Come the Clowns* in December 1938, Dorothy Parker and Alan Campbell invited their friends at the Booth Theatre to come to the Algonquin for a midnight party, to celebrate. As the *Times* noted, "The Campbells invited all their friends, which meant pretty nearly all the notables of Broadway." General manager Frank Case counted 182 guests, who consumed a whopping 732 cocktails. Among the attendees were Tallulah Bankhead, Robert Benchley, Madge Evans, Edna Ferber, Fredric March, Gene Tunney, and Harold Ross. According to Case, the Campbells left a $50 tip but stiffed the Algonquin for the rest. The hotel sued for the balance, and a judge ordered the couple to pay $488 (about $8,000 today). To reporters who got wind of the suit, a red-faced Case said: "The hotel wanted the money, not me. It was all very friendly, all water over the dam. We just made up."

## BROCK PEMBERTON

It sounds like the plot to one of his Broadway hits: Hick conquers metropolis. But it really did happen that way. Brock Pemberton went from Kansas newspaperman to powerful Broadway producer, and became the father of the Tony Awards.

Ralph Brock Pemberton was born on December 14, 1885, in Leavenworth and grew up in Emporia, Kansas, where his father worked as a salesman. William Allen White, legendary editor of the *Emporia Gazette*, had known him since he was a boy, and, after Pemberton graduated from the University of Kansas, White hired him as a reporter. A dynamo on the tiny staff, Pemberton thrived under White's tutelage. The elder newspaperman had earned a national reputation for his provocative editorials, and, in the age-old way of newspaper employment, he spoke to a New York City editor on Pemberton's behalf.

As a young Broadway producer, Brock Pemberton had several hits. ◆ ◆ ◆

Young Pemberton booked a one-way ticket for Manhattan in 1910 and, after a 1,300-mile train trek, arrived on Newspaper Row to find that the position wasn't going to materialize. But as luck had it, someone gave him a note to hand to Franklin P. Adams, who was on the *Evening Mail* at the time. Just as F.P.A. would later stick out his neck for Benchley and Kaufman, he also got a job for Pemberton as a reporter.

After a few months Pemberton transferred to the drama department at the *Mail*. For his first assignment, he innocently reviewed a musical called *Everywoman* at the old Herald Square Theatre as if he were in Emporia rather than Gotham. The staff found his hayseed review backslappingly funny, and the edition became a collector's item—much to Pemberton's chagrin.

In 1911 he moved to the *World* drama desk, where he got to know the bustling theater business intimately. A few years later he was offered the assistant drama editor position at the *Times*, working under Woollcott, the paper's chief drama critic. In 1915, Pemberton married Margaret McCoy (who later worked as a costumer on her husband's shows). In 1917, producer Arthur Hopkins—one of the most successful theater bosses in the city—offered him a different kind of job. In his new career, Pemberton worked in every capacity, from set construction to directing.

Pemberton stayed with Hopkins for just three years, but he learned all the skills a producer needs. When Hopkins passed on a three-act comedy called *Enter Madame*, Pemberton asked to produce it. He directed it as well, taking the biggest gamble of his life, which paid off. The show ran for two years at the Garrick, and he became a newly minted Broadway producer at the age of thirty-five. Soon after, Pemberton tapped Zona Gale to adapt her bestseller *Miss Lulu Bett* into a play, which opened just after Christmas 1920. A smash success at the Belmont, the production won the Pulitzer for drama the following year.

When the Round Table began, Pemberton and his wife were living at **123 East 53rd Street** in a building since demolished. In 1922, the offices of **Pemberton Productions** were at **224 West 47th Street.** For a dozen years the couple lived at **115 East 53rd Street,** but during World War II they moved to a grand Turtle Bay apartment in the **Beekman Terrace at 455 East 51st Street.**

Pemberton carved out a thirty-year career in the theater business. He took on risky shows and had many hits and several flops. He brought out the first plays by Maxwell Anderson and Sidney Howard. He launched the stage careers of Claudette Colbert, Miriam Hopkins, Walter Huston, Fredric March, and more. In 1928 he lost $40,000 on a show but bounced back the following year with the light comedy *Strictly Dishon-orable*, which began a long association with actress-director Antoinette Perry. The pair had a string of hits, and back-stage gossip hinted that they also had a long-running romantic relationship. In 1939, Pemberton and Perry were among those who helped to form the American Theatre Wing, which put on the Stage Door Canteen shows for servicemen during World War II. After Perry's death in 1946, Pemberton pushed for the creation of the Ameri-can Theatre Wing's Antoinette Perry Awards for Excellence in Theatre—the Tony Awards.

Brock Pemberton's East 51st Street apartment overlooks the East River.

◆ ◆ ◆

## MURDOCK PEMBERTON

Without Murdock Pemberton, the Algonquin Round Table wouldn't have existed. The group may have lunched elsewhere—the Astor or the Knickerbocker—but it was Murdock's decision to go to the Algonquin in 1919.

Pemberton took John Peter Toohey and Alexander Woollcott to the hotel and kicked off the daily gatherings. There he became close friends with Harold Ross. When *The New Yorker* launched in 1925, Pemberton started a thirty-six-year association with the publica-tion, beginning with writing advertising copy. Then came light verse, thirty years of "Talk of the Town" pieces, as well as fiction, essays, and reporting. He was the magazine's first art critic, and he gained national fame for being an everyman in the art world.

Over the years, Murdock Pemberton's role in launching the Round Table has been overlooked.
◆ ◆ ◆

Murdock Albert Pemberton was born on April 6, 1888, in Emporia, Kansas, two years younger than Brock, and the youngest of their parents' four children. The Pemberton brothers became so famous that when their mother died in 1937, the Associated Press published an obituary of her that appeared in newspapers across the country.

In 1910 both brothers worked for *Emporia Gazette* editor William Allen White. Murdock left Emporia for stints on the *Kansas City Star* and *Philadelphia North American*. When Brock moved to New York, his younger brother followed. Brock stayed in journalism for a little while, but Murdock immediately fell in love with the theater and became a publicity man. By 1912 his name was making the society pages.

In April 1916, Pemberton married Helen K. Tower at **St. Luke's Episcopal at 285 Convent Avenue** in Hamilton Heights. Woollcott—who seems to have been a member of everyone's wedding party—served as one of the ushers. The newlyweds soon had two children, Katherine and Murdock Jr. Providing for his family kept Pemberton out of the war, and in June 1917 he was a publicity agent for Charles Dillingham at the Hippodrome Theatre. Pemberton was also a genius for getting the theater into the papers. In 1919 when the Round Table started meeting, Pemberton was living at **777 Lexington Avenue.**

He took to wearing wild, sometimes checked shirts. His unorthodox sartorial decisions invariably got him press. "Murdock Pemberton has not worn a white shirt in ten years," wrote O. O. McIntyre in 1938. "The gaudier the better." Harold Ross appointed him *The New Yorker*'s first art critic, and in that capacity he championed modern art, becoming friendly with scores of first-rate artists, including Alexander Calder and Isamu Noguchi.

Sculptures by Alexander Calder. Early in his career, Murdock Pemberton wrote, "Here is a young man who will go far." Calder gave him a mobile. ◆ ◆ ◆

A little more than a dozen years after marrying Helen Tower, he left her and their children and moved to **671 Lexington Avenue** with his mistress, Frances Mahan, an actress-dancer from the Hippodrome who was twenty years his junior. In 1936, the new couple lived at **55 West 46th Street** before moving to **500 West 112th Street,** across from the Cathedral of St. John the Divine. Pemberton joined the mid-century exodus from the city, renting the ramshackle house on Ruth Hale's Sabine Farm in Stamford, Connecticut. There he built an art studio, became a "Sunday painter," and got Broun into painting.

In 1947 Pemberton returned to Emporia for the first time in twenty years for *The New Yorker*. His report, under "Our Far-Flung Correspondents," detailed the local beef, martinis, and gossip. Pemberton continued writing professionally until the Sixties, when he fell on hard times.

## HAROLD ROSS

In life, Harold Ross was always something of a mystery to his friends and the public. He started his career as an itinerant newspaperman, bouncing from one end of the country to the other and cultivating a reputation as a roustabout and loose cannon. But in his thirties, when *The New Yorker* went from the brink of cancellation to cultural zeitgeist, he didn't take advantage of his newfound celebrity; he stayed in the shadows. Nonetheless, he had an outsize personality and almost cartoonish mannerisms. Janet Flanner described him as

> an eccentric, impressive man to look at or listen to, a big-boned Westerner from Colorado who talked in windy gusts that gave a sense of fresh weather to his conversation. His face was homely, with a pendant lower lip; his teeth were far apart, and when I first knew him, after the First World War, he wore his butternut-colored thick hair in a high, stiff pompadour, like some wild gamecock's crest.

Ross was born in Aspen, Colorado, on November 6, 1892. His father, an immigrant from Northern Ireland, worked as an engineer in the local silver mines. When he was a boy, the family moved to Salt Lake City, where he joined the West High School newspaper and fell in love with journalism. He dropped out to work on the *Telegram*, the city newspaper, getting hooked on police stations, saloons, and house fires. His father now ran a demolition business and wanted his son to work for him, but young Ross knew what he wanted: At the age of eighteen, he left home to become a freelance tramp reporter.

Ross took up drinking, chain-smoking, bad food, poker, and the hard life of a roving reporter with gusto. He worked from San Francisco to New Orleans, and even to the outskirts of New York City. He

Harold Ross around 1923. ◆ ◆ ◆

did stints on papers in Atlanta and Sacramento, and as hostilities in Europe dominated the headlines, Ross watched with interest. When America entered the war, Ross rushed to enlist in early 1917. He and his fellow soldiers in an engineering regiment were sent to Bordeaux as construction workers. There he realized that instead of fighting the Kaiser's men, he was going to be digging ditches. When he found out that the army was starting a newspaper for the troops, he legged it to Paris. Ross soon joined the staff of *Stars and Stripes*, and the sloppy-looking private who never polished his boots fit right in.

For the duration of the war, Ross served as a journalist. The staff picked the twenty-five-year-old to be the editor, giving him his first taste of being the boss. The paper was a hit with the troops and even turned a profit, which went to the US Treasury after the war. On the staff, Ross met two men who would play a big part in his future: Captain Franklin P. Adams and Sergeant Alexander Woollcott. Adams was on the staff only for a short period, but they became lifelong friends. Woollcott had a sticky personality, and he and Ross developed a begrudging friendship that lasted for more than two decades. The most important person whom Ross met in France, however, was Jane Grant.

When the war ended, Ross followed her back to Manhattan and took an apartment with army pal John T. Winterich, at **56 West 11th Street** in the Village. The men restarted their weekly poker game that had been wildly popular in Paris. Captain Frank Adams had named it the Thanatopsis Inside Straight and Pleasure Club, and the game lasted twenty years. In March 1920, fewer than six months later, Ross and Grant married. Woollcott made all the arrangements for the wedding—then sent them a bill for his services.

While Grant worked on the *Times*, Ross took various editorial jobs. When the Round Table first met in June 1919, Ross attended as Woollcott's guest. Here he met future *New Yorker* contributors, such as Marc Connelly and Dorothy Parker. After he died Parker remembered him thus:

> His improbabilities started with his looks. His long body only seemed to be basted together, his hair was quills upon the fretful porcupine, and his teeth were Stonehenge, his clothes looked as if they had been brought up by somebody else. Expressions, sometimes several at a time, would race across his countenance, and always, especially when he thought no one was looking, not the brow alone but the whole expanse would be corrugated by his worries, his worries over his bitch-mistress, his magazine. But what he did and what he caused to be done with *The New Yorker* left his mark and his memory upon his times.

Ross and Grant lived with Heywood Broun and Ruth Hale during the summer of 1920. Then, for two years, they resided above a machine shop at **231 West 58th Street,** near Columbus Circle. When the couple scraped together enough money, they purchased a house that became legendary in literary and theatrical circles: **412 West 47th Street.**

In 1924, Ross and Grant developed a proposed "humorous weekly" magazine, relentlessly showing the mock-up to investors and contributors. Eventually the pieces fell into place, and in the summer of 1924 they secured offices at **25 West 45th Street.** Ross was in business.

The magazine had a rocky start, but Ross's vision never wavered. Among the early editors was Stanley Walker, legendary *Herald Tribune* city editor, who worked alongside Ross. Walker wrote that *The New Yorker* "demonstrated that a smart, casual style, coupled with a sophisticated viewpoint, does anything but repel the reader. . . . It has made money by treating its readers, not as pathological cases or a congregation of oafs, but as fairly intelligent persons who want information and entertainment."

Ross toiled like a workhorse on the magazine for the next quarter of a century. He ran his health into the ground and gave himself ulcers, stomach problems, and high blood pressure. His marriage to Grant suffered, and, like so many other couples associated with the Vicious Circle, they split. In 1930, following the divorce, Ross rented an apartment at **277 Park Avenue,** ten minutes from the office. It didn't last long: He violated his lease by having "persons of the opposite sex" as overnight guests, and was asked to leave. Ross took solace in poker and fishing trips, always trying to avoid the high life that his magazine extolled.

His second marriage came in 1934 to Marie Françoise "Frances" Elie, a Frenchwoman twenty years his junior. The couple had a daughter, Patricia, in 1935, but the marriage lasted fewer than five years. He remarried, for the third and final time, in 1940. Ross was forty-eight years old, and Ariane Allen, a party girl and failed actress-model, was twenty-five. The couple split their time between an apartment at **375 Park Avenue** and Ross's house in Stamford.

In life he toiled and struggled, but in death Ross entered the pantheon of American editors, considered one of the greatest of the twentieth century.

## ARTHUR H. SAMUELS

A member of the Vicious Circle who has fallen into obscurity, Arthur H. Samuels was a musician, reporter, editor, and publicity genius who helped Ross and Grant launch *The New Yorker*. Ross, who abhorred personal conflict, infamously fired him via cablegram while Samuels was on an ocean liner. Samuels went on to edit

*Harper's Bazaar,* poaching some of Ross's best talent. With a beautiful wife who was a retired silent-film star, Samuels was a fixture on the city gossip pages.

In early 1934 columnist O. O. McIntyre wrote:

> Samuels is blond and one of the few chieftains of the editorial sanctum with real musical ability. . . . Samuels was a pianist of concert caliber. His repertory ranges from his own back-room arrangement of "Frankie and Johnny" to the most difficult Bach. He is in his thirties and one of the few able to winnow a story or poem from the coy and reluctant Dot Parker.

Samuels was born on April 15, 1888, in Hartford, Connecticut. His father died when he was a boy, and he supported his mother. He worked his way through Princeton, and moved to New York in 1909, becoming a reporter at the *New York Sun* and traveling with former president Theodore Roosevelt as the paper's special correspondent. On the *Sun* he met Frank Sullivan, also a beat reporter, who became his best friend. From 1913 to 1917, he lived in Philadelphia and worked as the publicity manager of the Curtis Publishing

A savvy editor and sharp publicity man, Arthur Samuels was another of the Round Table men who married a movie star. ◆ ◆ ◆

Company in Independence Square. During the war he moved to Washington to work as an editor for the Food Administration. There he took charge of publicity for the Surgeon General's office, raising awareness about better treatment for wounded soldiers and Marines.

Samuels returned to Manhattan after the war, and for almost a decade was a partner in an advertising agency. When the Round Table began in 1919, he was thirty years old and well liked by all. An accomplished pianist and amateur composer, he wrote the score to the 1923 musical comedy *Poppy* for W. C. Fields and Madge Kennedy. The show ran at the old **Apollo Theatre at 223 West 42nd Street** for 350 performances, and Samuels made a tidy sum from the sheet music sales.

When Grant and Ross were getting *The New Yorker* off the ground, they turned to Samuels to write advertising copy and marketing materials. His successful publicity campaign drew attention to the new magazine in 1925, with testimonials from happy readers such as Irving Berlin, George Gershwin, and Al Jolson. Sales soared. From their days together at Princeton, Samuels knew publisher Raoul Fleischmann, who brought the publicity guru on board as an associate editor and penny-pincher. Ross usually enjoyed working with former newspapermen, but he didn't like the cozy relationship between Samuels and Fleischmann, forcing his rival out.

In February 1926, Samuels married actress Vivian Martin at the home of Neysa McMein. A gorgeous redhead, Martin had acted onstage and in silent movies for Paramount, and was seen as a rival to Mary Pickford. In 1927 they lived at **10 East 85th Street;** in 1930 they lived at **10 East 80th Street**, a stone's throw from the Met.

In 1930, William Randolph Hearst made Samuels editor of *Home & Field*, and a year later moved him to run *Harper's Bazaar*. Samuels had terrific rapport with writers, and got Dorothy Parker to submit some of her best short fiction to his magazine, such as "Dusk before Fireworks" and "Horsie."

## ROBERT E. SHERWOOD

When Dorothy Parker and Robert Benchley had lunch with coworker Robert E. Sherwood in 1919, they probably had no idea that the six-foot-seven young man sitting with them would surpass them in critical acclaim. As the three had coffee at the Algonquin, no one could have predicted that Sherwood, then twenty-three years old, would win four Pulitzer Prizes and an Oscar.

Of Robert E. Sherwood, the *Times* said, "He was often called 'idealist' and 'dreamer,' but there could be no reproach in such terms. He assumed the burdens of what he saw as his duty with constant courage." ◆ ◆ ◆

A supremely gifted writer, Sherwood could turn out snappy comedy pieces and silly songs or searing dramas that addressed intolerance and persecution. He was close friends with Irving Berlin and President Franklin D. Roosevelt, and he always maintained an easy grace and warmth that kept his friends close and his enemies disarmed.

Robert Emmet Sherwood was born in New Rochelle, New York, on April 4, 1896, the fourth of five children. His father was a stockbroker and his mother a distant relative of Irish patriot Robert Emmet, for whom the boy was named. He grew up in a large house at **251 Lexington Avenue,** summering in Westport, a tiny town upstate on Lake Champlain. In 1909 he went off to Milton Academy, outside Boston, where he was a poor student. Like his father, he went to Harvard, where he repeated his poor academic achievements. Sherwood spent his free time on drama and writing and was a member of the *Harvard Lampoon.*

When America entered the Great War, the US Army told him he was too tall to enlist. (He joked that the trenches would need to be dug even deeper for him.) So in 1916 he hopped a train to Montreal and joined the 5th Royal Highlanders, the famous Black Watch regiment, of the Canadian Army—kilt and all. He spent five and a half months in France as a private, fought in the trenches, took part in hand-to-hand combat, and twice was gassed by the Germans. During a major offensive, he was wounded and spent six months recovering, returning to New York in the spring of 1919 after peace was declared.

Sherwood arrived at a perfect time. Frank Crowninshield, who knew Sherwood's family socially, was the right-hand man to Condé Nast. Crowninshield enjoyed a parody of *Vanity Fair* that Sherwood edited at the *Harvard Lampoon*, which also produced his new managing editor, Benchley. The magazine's drama critic was Dorothy Parker, and the trio became fast friends and charter members of the Vicious Circle.

Sherwood's tenure at *Vanity Fair* lasted just six months, though, ending when Parker was fired and he and Benchley resigned in protest. Sherwood had no trouble finding a new job at *Life*, a humorous weekly at the time, for which Adams, Benchley, Broun, Parker, and others wrote. When movies were still silent, Sherwood became one of the country's pioneering film critics. One of his pieces reviewed cowboy actor Tom Mix: "They say he rides like part of the horse, but they don't say what part."

He may have had professional success galore, but Sherwood's personal life was a shambles. In October 1922, he married actress Mary Brandon at the **Little Church around the Corner, 1 East 29th Street,** with Douglas Fairbanks and Mary Pickford in the wedding party. The couple had one daughter, also named Mary. Sherwood divorced Brandon in 1934 and married Marc Connelly's ex-wife, Madeline Hurlock, a former silent-film star, in Budapest in June 1935.

Eventually Sherwood pulled away from the group to focus on more serious work. While working at *Life* he started writing plays. "In 1928 I left *Life*, primarily because I was fired, and became a playwright," Sherwood said. By the Thirties, he had hit his stride. He won three Pulitzers for Broadway hits *Idiot's Delight* (1936), *Abe Lincoln in Illinois* (1939), and *There Shall Be No Night* (1941). Then he went to Hollywood and found success there, too. He was nominated for an Oscar for writing *Rebecca* (1940), and won in 1946 for *The Best Years of Our Lives*.

## LAURENCE STALLINGS

The Round Table considered Laurence Stallings a hero because of his sacrifices as a Marine in World War I. That combat experience provided inspiration for a best-selling book, a gritty Broadway drama, magazine stories and fiction, and a hit silent film.

Stallings was born on November 25, 1894, in Macon, Georgia. He graduated from Wake Forest, and his first job was as a reporter on the *Atlanta Constitution*

As a writer, Laurence Stallings always had one subject to tackle: wartime experiences. ◆ ◆ ◆

in 1915. Two years later he enlisted in the Marines and was sent to France, where he participated in some of the bloodiest campaigns of the war. He received a battlefield commission and took command of a Marine outfit. In June 1918, at the Battle of Belleau Wood near the Marne, Stalling was wounded. Awarded the Purple Heart and the Croix de Guerre, he spent eight months recovering in France before being shipped home after the armistice was signed.

Once home, he married his college sweetheart, Helen Poteat, daughter of Wake Forest president William Louis Poteat. The wedding took place on campus in Winston-Salem. Afterward, the couple moved to Washington, D.C., where Stallings joined the *Washington Times* as a reporter and earned his master's degree from Georgetown. His writing career was taking off, but he never fully recovered from his combat injuries. In 1922 his right leg was amputated.

After recuperating, Stallings and his wife moved to New York, where he joined the *World*. A tall, dark-haired, handsome Southerner, he sometimes came to the Algonquin wearing his artificial leg, other times on a crutch. Coworkers Heywood Broun and Deems Taylor introduced him to the Vicious Circle after it was an established institution.

In 1924 Stallings was writing book reviews three days a week for the *World*. Executive editor Herbert Bayard Swope tapped him to join the op-ed page with Adams, Broun, Sullivan, and Woollcott. He shared an office with Maxwell Anderson, a fellow editorial writer at the time. They collaborated on their first play, *What Price Glory?*, for the powerful Broadway producer Arthur Hopkins, who also had staged Don Marquis's hit play *The Old Soak*. With *What Price Glory?*, Stallings shared his real-life experiences of the trauma and heartbreak

Three *New York World* columnists on vacation; from left, Laurence Stallings, Deems Taylor, and on the right, Franklin P. Adams. Between Taylor and Adams is Helen Stallings. ◆ ◆ ◆

experienced by soldiers in combat. It was a hit at the **Plymouth The-atre, 236 West 45th Street,** and ran for more than a year.

His novel *Plumes* was a finalist for the 1925 Pulitzer Prize, but another Algonquin regular, Edna Ferber, and her novel *So Big* edged it out. His novel was adapted into *The Big Parade* that year, and was among the first blockbusters in the silent-film era. Directed by maverick filmmaker King Vidor, *The Big Parade* played to sellout crowds across the nation. A railroad car transported the orchestra, lighting, and personnel from town to town. Made just seven years after the conflict, the film was the first to show the gritty side of the war on the big screen. The central character, played by John Gilbert, loses a leg in battle, like Stallings.

Stallings and his wife had two children together. In December 1936, she sued him for divorce in Reno, Nevada, charging him with cruelty. In a private trial, the judge granted the divorce that ended their troubled seventeen-year union. Stallings walked away from his family and estate in North Carolina and never saw either again. He married Louisa St. Leger Vance, a twenty-five-year-old writer, in March 1937 at her parents' home at **410 East 57th Street.** They had two children. Stallings moved to Hollywood, where he remained for the rest of his life.

## Donald Ogden Stewart

A small-town kid, Donald Ogden Stewart grew up to win an Oscar and become close friends with Ernest Hemingway, Katharine Hepburn, and Paul Robeson. A man of unswerving convictions about freedom of speech and personal liberty, he had an FBI file more than 1,500 pages thick. Director J. Edgar Hoover personally alerted the US attorney general that undercover agents were tailing the writer. Stewart got into such hot water during the communist witch hunt

Donald Ogden Stewart and his girlfriend, actress Patsy Ruth Miller, in 1925. ◆ ◆ ◆

that his passport was torn up, and he lived the last thirty years of his life in exile in London.

Stewart was born on November 30, 1894, in Columbus, Ohio, the son of a local attorney, later a judge. In 1909 the family shipped him to Phillips Exeter Academy, where he took up writing, ultimately becoming editor of the school newspaper. He entered Yale with the class of 1916 and made the Skull and Bones society. When he graduated, he avoided military service by working in corporate America, bouncing between Chicago, New York, Minneapolis, and Pittsburgh. In Minnesota he befriended another dreamer, F. Scott Fitzgerald, who urged Stewart to speak to his friends at *Vanity Fair*.

Through Fitzgerald, Stewart met the magazine's assistant editor, Edmund Wilson. He liked a parody that Stewart had written in the style of Theodore Dreiser and bought it. Stewart instantly became a magazine writer. Over several months, he wrote more parodies of popular writers, including his pal Fitzgerald. After falling in with Benchley and Parker, he joined the Round Table.

In 1922, Stewart and his mother, Clara, rented an apartment at **6 Minetta Street.** When he wasn't living there, he stayed at the **Yale Club, 50 Vanderbilt Avenue.** At the time he was writing for *Harper's Bazaar,* its offices located at **119 West 40th Street.**

Like Benchley and Ring Lardner, Stewart's style came to be called "crazy humor" for the wild non sequiturs and nonsense writing. "Dorothy Parker was particularly encouraging," Stewart recalled years later. "That was one of Dorothy's great gifts. She always made you feel like she was on your side, particularly against critics. And if you had a hangover, Dotty always pretended to have a worse one." Stewart celebrated his twenty-ninth birthday at Parker's apartment with Irving Berlin and a bottle of champagne; he claimed the two helped write the last lines of Berlin's "What'll I Do?"

In 1927 Stewart married Beatrice Ames. Connelly was an usher and Benchley his best man at the Montecito, California, wedding—though Benchley had broken his leg at the bachelor party by falling down a flight of stairs. The Stewarts traveled in high style and, like their friend Dottie Parker, they preferred French Line. In 1935 they sailed on the SS *Normandie,* the largest and fastest ship in the world.

Stewart turned to writing plays about the same time that the Round Table ran out of gas. In the Thirties, he moved to Hollywood and became a highly paid screenwriter. He involved himself in left-wing politics around the same time as Parker, but much more deeply. He went from being the life of the party to joining the Communist Party. Later he was elected president of the Hollywood Anti-Nazi League, making headlines not for writing the new Norma Shearer–Tyrone Power picture, but for speaking against fascism. The highlight of his Hollywood career came when he adapted *The Philadelphia Story* from his friend Philip Barry's play, winning the Oscar for the screenplay in 1941 with Dalton Trumbo, another left-wing writer. Through these new friends, however, he alienated a lot of old ones. He left his wife for journalist Ella Winter, a communist and the widow of muckraker Lincoln Steffens.

He didn't know it at the time, but his last view of America was of New York City through the porthole of a steamship. In 1951 he and Winter went to London to produce a play. He did little work for the rest of his life, and never saw the United States again.

## FRANK SULLIVAN

Aleck Woollcott reported to the Round Table one day that he had just spoken to "ten thousand women in St. Paul."

"What did you tell them?" Frank Sullivan asked. "No?"

That was Sullivan's forte: humor with the lightest touch. Beloved by the group for his charming wit and marvelous writing style, he was never mean or spiteful in his work, which poked fun at modern

Frank Sullivan kept up a lifetime of correspondence with his friends. ◆ ◆ ◆

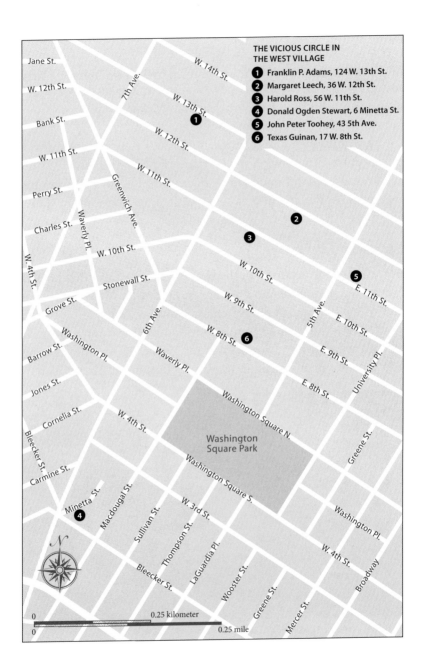

THE VICIOUS CIRCLE IN
THE WEST VILLAGE

1 Franklin P. Adams, 124 W. 13th St.
2 Margaret Leech, 36 W. 12th St.
3 Harold Ross, 56 W. 11th St.
4 Donald Ogden Stewart, 6 Minetta St.
5 John Peter Toohey, 43 5th Ave.
6 Texas Guinan, 17 W. 8th St.

Washington
Square Park

0        0.25 kilometer
0        0.25 mile

life by skewering it gently. He contributed to *The New Yorker* for fifty years, starting with the fifth issue, writing the Christmas greeting from 1932 to 1974. Some of his 1933 holiday greeting:

> *Hail, Yuletide, merry and jolly,*
> *Season of mistletoe, Santa, and holly!*
> *Hail, Christmas, day of joy!*
> *And hail, while you're up, to Myrna Loy!*
> *(You can't fool me with these Christmas rhymes,*
> *I've written them all far too many times.)*
> *So hail, Noel, I thee greet.*
> *Hail, rain, snow, and sleet.*
> *Oozing affability from every pore,*
> *I greet Toscanini and Friedrich Schorr;*
> *I greet my friends and I greet my foes;*
> *I greet Fanny Brice and Billy Rose.*
> *Only a wet smack could be miffed*
> *On such a day as Dec. 25th.*

Frank Sullivan was born on September 22, 1892, in Saratoga Springs, New York. As a kid he worked at the racetrack, bringing water to high-class spectators. After graduating from Cornell, he returned home, and his first newspaper job was as a young reporter on *The Saratogian*, making $7 a week. After World War I, he found work in New York on the *Herald* and the *Evening Sun*, and in the early Twenties he landed on the city desk of the *World*. His career almost came to a crashing halt the night he was writing an obituary, incorrectly reporting that a well-known society woman had died. He tried to resign, but editor Herbert Bayard Swope assigned him to write humor pieces instead. Shortly thereafter Sullivan was sharing space with Adams, Broun, Stallings, Taylor, and Woollcott.

Sullivan created Mr. Arbuthnot, a character used many times in his pieces and an alleged expert on clichés. Sullivan cross-examined Mr. Arbuthnot and spun elaborate hackneyed exchanges such as this one:

Q: What do you do for exercise?
A: I play the game. And hang up records. I sail a little?
Q: A skiff?
A: No, under false colors. I box some, too, hitting below the belt, and I go in for dancing.

Sullivan never married; the longest trip he ever took was to Boston. When the *World* folded in 1932, he could have stayed in New York and become a radio-show gag writer, joined a magazine staff, or tried his hand at Hollywood, where almost every one of his friends went. Instead, Sullivan returned home to Saratoga Springs and remained there for the rest of his life, working as a freelancer.

## DEEMS TAYLOR

Who was the Round Table member so famous that he made the cover of *Time* in 1931? Who wrote the country's first great opera? Who shared billing with Mickey Mouse in *Fantasia* but his music is rarely performed today?

If jazz or rock 'n' roll had never come along, today's audiences might still recognize Deems Taylor's name. A brilliant, intelligent, witty man, he was a nineteenth century–style composer trapped in the Jazz Age. But because he composed classical music and operas, his relevance flickered out, and he spent his last decades in relative obscurity. Yet from one world war through the other, his influence in the music world was immense.

Taylor was one of the few Round Table members that claimed a New York City birthright. Joseph Deems Taylor was born at **152 West 17th Street** on December 22, 1885. The name Deems came from his father's favorite pastor. In elementary school he took piano lessons, almost the only musical instruction Taylor ever undertook. He wrote his first composition, a waltz, when he was ten. As a boy, his family moved to **2275 Loring Place** in the Bronx, and as an adult Taylor returned to live there when he

A lifelong New Yorker, Deems Taylor's career in music spanned sixty years. ◆ ◆ ◆

ran out of money. In 1896 Taylor entered the Ethical Culture School for his high school education.

Taylor's life in the arts began at New York University. He loved music, books, and the theater, and tried to combine all three. He scored four years of collegiate shows. He graduated in 1906 with a taste for show business and an eye on Broadway. He tried writing classical scores and compositions to limited success. His college work caught the attention of major league producers, so he wrote Broadway shows, but his heart belonged to classical music. In 1913 he won a prize for his symphonic poem "The Siren Song," which spurred him in that direction.

In September 1910, Taylor married Jane Anderson, an aspiring magazine writer. The wedding took place at the **Fordham Reformed Church, 2705 Reservoir Avenue,** in the Kingsbridge neighborhood

The Paterno opened in 1909, and Taylor moved in soon after. ◆ ◆ ◆

of the Bronx. The newlyweds then moved into an apartment at **The Paterno,** a grand building at **440 Riverside Drive,** near Columbia University. Taylor was struggling to make a living as a composer. Broadway was changing, and tastes were running to comedies and operettas, two styles that didn't suit him. He took a job in public relations and composed on the side.

Taylor contributed to Franklin P. Adams's newspaper columns, signing his pieces "SMEED," his name spelled backward. In 1916 he came into contact with future members of the Vicious Circle. F.P.A. deemed him the year's best contributor to his column; a raucous congratulatory dinner took place at **Scheffel Hall,** an old German *rathskeller* at **190 Third Avenue** on the Lower East Side. Robert Benchley served as guest speaker.

With the war brewing, Taylor's wife left him and sailed to England to become a freelance war correspondent. With F.P.A.'s help, Taylor joined the *Tribune*, which also employed Benchley, Broun, and Kaufman. Taylor took to newspaper work with gusto. When hostilities erupted, he went to France to be a correspondent himself—but his six months there shook him up. Taylor reunited with his wife, but the marriage was over.

He returned to New York and composed one of his greatest works, *Through the Looking Glass*, a musical suite based on *Alice's Adventures in Wonderland* by Lewis Carroll. The New York Chamber Music Society premiered it in February 1919 at **Aeolian Hall, 29 West 42nd Street,** a thousand-seat concert hall second in stature only to Carnegie Hall. Critical acclaim finally came. At the time, Taylor lived at **32 East 28th Street.**

He then took a position offered by Herbert Bayard Swope, executive editor of the *World*. Taylor soon proved himself a knowledgeable critic, and his commentary set new standards in journalism for music criticism. He split his time composing and writing about music.

His next goal was the loftiest of all: to compose an opera for the Metropolitan Opera House. Taylor asked Edna St. Vincent Millay to write the libretto, and the two made a fantastic team. *The King's Henchman*, a medieval fantasy, premiered in 1927 and was the toast of the town, the first successful American opera written in English. The Met performed it three seasons in a row, a rare occurrence. Taylor found himself in demand to lecture on music and to be a radio commentator.

When Taylor was basking at the height of his *King's Henchman* fame, he reveled in the top echelon of New York celebrities. One letter from Paris reached him, addressed as follows:

> Deems Taylor, Esq.
> Somewhere in New York City
> Try *Vanity Fair* or the Metropolitan Opera House
> or just stand at 42nd Street and yell his name . . .
> someone will tell you where he lives.

On February 16, 1931, *Time* magazine featured Deems Taylor on its cover, in profile, at his piano, writing on a composition page.

Behind closed doors, however, Taylor's personal life was difficult. After his first marriage ended, he tried twice more. Those, too, ended in divorce court. In 1947 he and his third wife, a teenager, lived at **2 East 60th Street.**

## John Peter Toohey

The sole claim to fame of public relations master John Peter Toohey is that he gave *The New Yorker* its name. For this deed, Harold Ross gave him $1,500 in company stock. But Toohey also acted as press agent for numerous Broadway classics, including those from pal George S. Kaufman: *Dinner at Eight, You Can't Take It with You*, and *The Man Who Came to Dinner*. Toohey was with Murdock Pemberton when the latter led Aleck Woollcott to the Algonquin for the debut luncheon, and was considered the founder of the marathon poker games held on the second floor, called the Thanatopsis Inside Straight and Pleasure Club.

Toohey was born on September 18, 1879, in Binghamton, New York, the son of Irish immigrants. His career started in Pennsylvania

The Thanatopsis Inside Straight and Pleasure Club poker table in 1939. Clockwise from bottom left: Heywood Broun, Harold Ross, John Peter Toohey, F.P.A., George S. Kaufman, Alexander Woollcott, John Winterich, and Robert Sherwood. ◆ ◆ ◆

on the *Scranton Tribune*. After the turn of the century, he joined the *Washington Post* as a reporter. Shortly thereafter he moved to Manhattan, where he joined the famed editorial staff of the *New York Evening World*. There he met many friends from the writing and theater world. He quit journalism to enter the growing field of press representation on Broadway. At the time—with nearly eighty theaters in operation—there was plenty of work to go around. He first worked as a manager for the Shubert Organization, traveling to Ohio, Indiana, and Minnesota with road companies from about

1910 to 1915. Toohey also managed big musicals, including *The Jolly Bachelors* and *The Sun Dodgers*.

Toohey married Viola Latham before World War I; the couple had one son, John Latham, who later followed his father into the business. From 1918 to 1925 they lived at **526 West 111th Street.** He left the road to work in New York for powerful theater bosses Klaw & Erlanger. From 1920 to 1942 he worked for influential producer Sam H. Harris.

In his spare time, Toohey wrote short stories, basing his pieces on what he knew best. He sold several to *Collier's* and the *Saturday Evening Post*—including "Pie for the Press Agent" and "Jimmy Aids the Uplift"—at the same time he was helping to launch the Round Table. He also tried his hand as a playwright, collaborating on half a dozen shows. Among his earliest, *Swifty* (1922) starred a twenty-one-year-old actor named Humphrey Bogart. Toohey also collaborated with Anne Morrison on *Jonesy*, a hit dramatization of his short stories.

From short stories he branched out into novels, his subject matter again drawn from his own career. *Fresh Every Hour* (1922) was about a press agent and an amateur actress. Most accounts say Toohey was portly, fun-loving, and irrepressible. Like F.P.A. and Marc Connelly, he belonged to the **Players Club, 16 Gramercy Park South.** He also was an early member of the Dutch Treat Club, which still meets at the **National Arts Club at 15 Gramercy Park South.** Toohey and his family lived nearby, at **43 Fifth Avenue**, just south of Union Square.

It was generally accepted that he was the first Vicious Circle member to visit a psychiatrist, happily relating details of his sessions over lunch to friends. Toohey got uproarious laughter, if little help, from therapy. From the Thirties to the Forties, Toohey was one of the most in-demand publicity men on Broadway. In 1939, when

Kaufman wrote *The Man Who Came to Dinner* with Moss Hart, he asked Toohey to be the press representative. To Toohey's delight, the show skewered his friend of twenty-five years, Woollcott.

## DAVID H. WALLACE

Theatrical press agent Dave Wallace counted among his successes working with Robert E. Sherwood on his 1927 hit *The Road to Rome*, a three-act play with Philip Merivale as Hannibal and Jane Cowl as Amytis. Through Wallace, the men of the Round Table encountered a hot commodity: hungry young actresses. Wallace was the man to know if you wanted to meet women auditioning for, or already cast in, new shows.

David Harold Wallace was born on September 22, 1888, in Syracuse, New York. His father was a Presbyterian ministers, and as a boy, he lived in Holton, Kansas, where his father preached. At Syracuse University he developed an interest in drama and wrote the varsity show. After graduating, he went to work as a reporter for the Syracuse *Herald*. But Wallace loved the stage, so he moved to New York in 1912 and started writing theater reviews for the *Morning Telegraph*, where he

In 1931 David H. Wallace lived in this handsome building at 6 East 8th Street in the Village. ◆ ◆ ◆

met Broun and Connelly. As many Round Tablers did, Wallace then moved from newspapers to behind the scenes on Broadway.

In June 1917, he was working as advertising and publicity manager for the William A. Brady Company, Brady being a former actor turned Broadway director and theater owner. Wallace worked in theater publicity during Broadway's golden age. He counted Ethel Barrymore, John Barrymore, and Laurette Taylor as personal clients. He also worked as company manager on numerous shows, including *What Price Glory?*, cowritten by friend Laurence Stallings. As many Round Tablers also did, he wrote several plays, including *Rope* (1928), about a lynching in a small Tennessee town.

A devoted poker player and regular member of Thanatopsis, Wallace was among the first members of the Vicious Circle. In 1931, after the group had wound down, he lived at **6 East 8th Street** in the Village.

## JOHN V. A. WEAVER

John V. A. Weaver was discovered by H. L. Mencken. ◆ ◆ ◆

If Dorothy Parker was the reigning wit of the Vicious Circle, then John V. A. Weaver was her polar opposite. Both were the same age; both wrote poetry, short stories, criticism, plays, and screenplays. Parker is remembered as the quotable good-time girl, yet Weaver, who had a greater output and a modicum of fame at the time, isn't remembered for anything. He married a fellow member, actress Peggy Wood, and was friendly with the whole group. In fewer than ten years, he went from unknown poet to the screenwriter who put words into the mouth of silent-screen superstar Louise Brooks in her first talking picture.

John Van Alstyn Weaver was born on July 17, 1893, in Charlotte, North Carolina, but grew up in Winnetka, Illinois. He graduated from Hamilton College in upstate New York. Classmate and author Carl Carmer said: "John Weaver had impact. Meeting him meant feeling the smack of a personality . . . Weaver had an inquisitive mind, practically no tact, and an embarrassing directness."

Weaver attended Harvard for one semester after Hamilton, and before moving to Chicago to write advertising copy and book reviews for the *Daily News*. From 1917 to 1919 he served in the army ordnance corps at Camp Hancock in Augusta, Georgia.

A turning point in Weaver's life came in 1919 when he read H. L. Mencken's *The American Language* and took issue with the Baltimore pundit's assertion that slang couldn't be taken seriously, and that real writers didn't use the language of the streets. Weaver wrote in protest, whereupon Mencken challenged him, if he thought it could be done, to try. Weaver's response was "Élégie Américaine," which read in part:

> *Oh God! I don't see how I ever stand it!*
> *He was so big and strong! He was a darb!*
> *The swellest dresser, with them nifty shirts*
> *That fold down, and them lovely nobby shoes,*
> *And always all his clothes would be one color,*
> *Like green socks with green ties, and a green hat,*
> *And everything . . . We never had no words*
> *Or hardly none . . . And now to think that mouth*
> *I useta kiss is bitin' into dirt,*
> *And through them curls I useta smooth a bullet*

*Has went . . .*
*I wisht it would of killed me, too.*

Mencken loved it and sent Weaver $11.25 to publish it in *The Smart Set*, a leading literary magazine of the era. Publisher Alfred A. Knopf took note and asked the twenty-seven-year-old if he had enough material for a book. *In American* (1921) resulted, a bestseller that had seven printings in its first year in print.

Weaver moved to New York in 1920 and was immediately befriended by Woollcott, also a Hamilton alum. Woollcott brought the aspiring poet to the Algonquin and introduced him to the table. Weaver's star quickly rose, and literary critics dubbed him the man who "wrote in the American language." As early as 1921, Weaver was mentioned in the same literary columns as Sherwood Anderson, Theodore Dreiser, and Eugene O'Neill.

From 1920 to 1924 Weaver held a day job as the literary editor of the *Brooklyn Daily Eagle*, working alongside Ruth Hale and William Murray. During this time, while a member of the Round Table, Weaver wrote some of his best poetry. His other books of verse were *Finders* (1923), *More in American* (1926), *To Youth* (1927), *Turning Point* (1930), and *Trial Balance* (1931).

In 1926, he collaborated with George Abbott to write the comedy *Love 'Em and Leave 'Em*, his sole Broadway hit, which ran for two hundred performances. Critics now called him the "slang poet" who wrote in "Americanese." That same year, the play became the hit movie starring nineteen-year-old Louise Brooks in one of her first roles.

Weaver went to Hollywood to write for King Vidor, but the work didn't fulfill him, and he earned fewer than a dozen screenplay credits.

Weaver met Peggy Wood at the Algonquin. The pair hit it off, and dated while she traveled with road companies of various stage shows. The engagement lasted more than three years, and they wed in 1924. Not long after their only child was born, Weaver contracted tuberculosis. Gravely ill, he left Los Angeles and moved to Colorado for the mountain air. There he finished his final screenplay, adapting Mark Twain's *The Adventures of Tom Sawyer* for producer David O. Selznick.

## Peggy Wood

She starred in every acting genre in popular culture in the twentieth century: Broadway, radio, television, silent pictures, and the talkies. Peggy Wood began her career as an ingenue in a little theater on Broadway. She was among the first TV stars. Audiences last saw her as the Mother Abbess in *The Sound of Music* in 1965, for which she received a nomination for an Academy Award for best supporting actress. Wood had an indomitable spirit and a

Peggy Wood liked to say she was the first actress admitted to the Round Table. ◆ ◆ ◆

drive to succeed in roles from Shakespeare to Coward. She wasn't a stunning beauty and was rarely a leading lady, yet she carved out a niche for herself as a dependable journeyman actor, whom audiences liked. Between roles she wrote, turning out magazine articles about acting and books about life onstage.

She was born in Brooklyn on February 9, 1892, and grew up at **650 Prospect Place** in Bedford-Stuyvesant. Her father, Eugene Wood, was a writer for popular magazines and the *World*. As a girl she took singing, acting, and dancing lessons. Her goal: the stage. At the age of eighteen, she made her professional Broadway debut in the chorus of *Naughty Marietta*, an operetta, earning $20 a week. In the audience, her father exclaimed, "My God! Look at Margaret Wood!" From that point on, she appeared regularly on Broadway and in traveling stage companies across the country.

Briefly engaged to actor Otto Kruger, she was living at **1196 Park Avenue** in 1918. When the Vicious Circle began the following year, she had been treading the boards for almost ten years, and she liked to say that she was the first actress brought to a lunch—and by Woollcott. Unlike other actresses invited to the table, Wood, a known figure and welcome addition, held her own. Years later, when she was starring in Noël Coward's *Bitter Sweet*, Harpo Marx said: "Why didn't you tell me you were as good as this? I'd have married you long ago!"

At the Algonquin Wood met John V. A. Weaver, recently arrived from Chicago. *Vanity Fair* had just published an anti-love poem that he had written, so of course she tried to charm him. Her charm worked, and they started a secret, two-year romance. But while Wood acted and Weaver wrote, the stress of being apart caused Wood to lose her voice. The couple married on Valentine's Day, 1924, at Hamilton Cathedral during a cruise vacation to Bermuda. They honeymooned there for a month before returning to New York. Wood went back to Broadway, and Weaver worked at the *Brooklyn Daily Eagle* as literary editor. They lived at **68 Montague Street** in Brooklyn Heights after they were married; had a son, David; and a year after their wedding, bought property in rural Stamford, Connecticut.

After Weaver's sudden death in 1938, Wood continued to live in Stamford and in a pied-à-terre at **400 East 49th Street,** later marrying printing executive William A. Walling. Her fame grew enormously when she starred on the CBS show *Mama*, about a family of Norwegian immigrants who came to America in the early 1900s. The show aired from 1949 to 1957 and was so popular that King Gustaf VI Adolf of Sweden awarded her a medal in 1953 and made her an honorary citizen.

Weaver and Wood lived on Montague Street in Brooklyn Heights after they married. ◆ ◆ ◆

## ALEXANDER WOOLLCOTT

If a sun shone at the center of the Round Table universe, it was Alexander Woollcott, around whom the rest of the members gravitated. Woollcott grandly accepted or rejected new additions to the table, but he also delivered catty remarks in a squeaky falsetto. Edna Ferber called him a "New Jersey Nero who mistook his pinafore for a toga." He had such a polarizing effect on those close to him that he was both beloved and loathed—often at the same time, by the same people. His first biographer received responses like this from Woollcott's old friends: "If there is a hell for important people who are causelessly cruel to the helpless and unimportant, I hope he is there." Another friend wrote, "I want no part of Woollcott, dead or alive."

Woollcott ranked among the most popular men of his era. His fame helped to sell automobiles and life insurance. He was drama critic for the *Times, Sun,* and the *World*; he wrote profiles—exclusively of chums—for *The New Yorker* and *McCall's*; he starred in CBS radio's *Town Crier* talk show; and he lives on today as the model for Sheridan Whiteside in Kaufman and Hart's *The Man Who Came to Dinner.* But as one wit summed him up, he was chiefly famous for being famous.

Woollcott loved this wartime portrait of himself by fellow *Stars and Stripes* member Leroy Baldridge so much that he gave reproductions to his friends. Much to their dismay he expected it to be displayed in a prominent location. ◆ ◆ ◆

The last of his parents' five children, Alexander Humphries Woollcott was born on January 19, 1887, on a commune called The Phalanx, in Colts Neck, New Jersey, founded before the Civil War. Perhaps as a result, Woollcott exhibited a lifelong fear of being alone, always craving companionship and communal living arrangements. His father was a rootless itinerant, and the family moved often. Even at a young age, Woollcott was large, ingratiating, and possessed of a peculiar falsetto voice. Once, when an elementary school bully picked on him, the future literary star shouted, "Stop, or I shall reveal the shameful secret of your birth!"

At Hamilton College in upstate New York, he took part in college shows and developed a love for writing. He played female roles in those collegiate theatricals, which led some to suspect he was homosexual, a charge he dodged his entire life. No evidence supports this, but he did live his whole life without intimate companions of either sex. After graduating from Hamilton, he moved to New York City.

The introverted young man landed in the city room of the *New York Times*, traversing the metropolis to witness fires and murder scenes. Being dispatched to Nova Scotia in April 1912 to report on the sinking of the RMS *Titanic* pushed him to the breaking point, however. The sight of the frozen corpses was too much for him. Soon after, he moved to the drama department, where he remained for the rest of his career.

Woollcott became a critic at age twenty-five and earned $60 a week. For years he wrote a column, "Second Thoughts on First Nights," which contained as much gossip as theater news. Two Round Table members, George S. Kaufman and Brock Pemberton, worked under him. He wrote his reviews with a flourish, but his caustic criticisms prompted the ire of more than one theater manager who banned Woollcott from his playhouse.

In 1916, Woollcott battled theater owners Sam and Lee Shubert to a standstill in the courts and eventually was allowed back in. But Woollcott knowingly and repeatedly crossed one particular line: He made a conscious effort to meet and ingratiate himself with actors and theater folk. He reveled in his role as a *Times* man, and throughout his career he curried favor with the very people he reviewed. If he had any journalistic ethics, he left them on the sidewalk before entering a Broadway theater. He wanted more for himself than just writing about the stars of the day; he also wanted to live a charmed life, to be their dinner companions and weekend guests.

Woollcott lived off his friends. An acquaintance became a magazine article. If the friend made for good copy, Woollcott sold the same story to several magazines—which infuriated Harold Ross. Woollcott was accused, to his face, of limiting his circle of friends to those who made good subjects for his *New Yorker* profiles. He glumly admitted it was true.

For twenty years, he was a constant presence in New York society. He was close to Jane Grant and Harold Ross, and lived with them at **412 West 47th Street** in 1922. He adored Harpo Marx, and takes fair credit for bringing the Marx Brothers to the attention of a wider audience in 1924. But he could be incredibly caustic and mean-spirited at times. When he moved into a new apartment in the **Hotel des Artistes, 1 West 67th Street,** he sent out a "shower" notice to his friends, requesting housewarming gifts of linen, china, and silver. F.P.A. sent him a handkerchief, a mustache cup, and a dime.

Woollcott never won a major literary award; his name never made any significant lists. But that didn't matter to the man from Colts Neck. During the war, President Roosevelt asked him to recommend good mysteries to read, and that remained one of Woollcott's most treasured honors.

Woollcott and the playwrights who gave him immortality onstage, Moss Hart and George S. Kaufman.

◆ ◆ ◆

# {3}

# THE ALGONQUIN HOTEL

## A Cultural Landmark

*Restraint is required to keep from being annoyed by queries as to what has become of the Round Table. What became of the reservoir at Fifth Avenue and 42nd Street? These things do not last forever.*

—FRANK CASE, OWNER, 1938

West Forty-fourth between Fifth and Sixth Avenues on which the Algonquin stands has hundreds of hotel beds, but the **Algonquin Hotel at 59–63 West 44th Street** stands out. For more than a century it has accommodated the intersection between the publishing and theater worlds, a favorite destination among writers and actors. The Algonquin carries on traditions passed down from owner to owner across the decades.

It isn't the oldest hotel on the block. Both the Royalton at number 44 and the Iroquois at number 49 opened in 1900. The Puritan Realty Company bought the Algonquin plot, 72 by 100 feet, for $180,000 in November 1901. The Thompson-Starrett Company built the 136-foot-tall building in just seven months. Puritan put up $500,000, and Thompson-Starrett acted as architects and contractors. Twenty-eight-year-old architect Goldwin Starrett worked on the hotel with his brothers Theodore, Ralph, and William.

The Algonquin Hotel is part of Club Row. ◆ ◆ ◆

It opened as the Hotel Algonquin, named for the Native Americans in New England during the pre-Colonial era. First owner Ann Stetson Foster chose "Algonquin" because the Hotel Iroquois stood next door. "It will make a veritable Indian settlement," she said.

The twelve-story hotel had 192 rooms and suites. The first guests checked in on November 22, 1902. An en suite room cost $2 a day, while a three-bedroom suite with private hall, sitting room, dining room, three bathrooms, and library set lodgers back $10. Originally it was intended to be a residential hotel, but it found more success with short-term guests. Following extensive renovations in 2012, the hotel now has 181 rooms, 25 of them suites.

Albert T. Foster and his wife, Ann Stetson Foster, were the Algonquin's first owners, and they controlled it for the shortest period of any of the hotel's eight ownership groups to date. Foster, a gambler, moved to town from Buffalo at the turn of the twentieth century with his wife. The couple jointly owned the Puritan Realty Company and had the lease on the neighboring Hotel Iroquois. Foster's stake in the new hotel came from a $50,000 loan from his wealthy wife. Not long after the Algonquin opened, Ann Foster left her husband, took their child, and sued him for ownership of the hotel. A judge appointed the hotel's manager, Frank Case, as one of the receivers to manage the property for the couple. In the end, Foster wound up with the lease and the full contents of the hotel, while the former Mrs. Foster got the building, forcing him out. After Foster lost the hotel, he developed homes in Westbury, Long Island.

The hotel changed hands in November 1903 when Dr. Andrew H. Smith, a retired physician and past president of the New York Academy of Medicine, and his son, Dr. Davison H. Smith, bought the Algonquin for about $500,000 from the Fosters. In 1910, at age seventy-three, Andrew Smith died in his apartment in the hotel. His family owned the hotel for close to twenty-five years.

# The Young Architect

When the first guest checked into the Algonquin, nobody was prouder than Goldwin Starrett, the young architect who designed it. He was born on September 29, 1874, in Lawrence, Kansas, but grew up in Chicago, one of five brothers, all of whom went into architecture, construction, and engineering. Starrett studied engineering at the University of Michigan and followed his two older brothers to a position with Daniel H. Burnham & Co. in Chicago. Starrett became one of Burnham's principal assistants.

Goldwin Starrett, architect. Suite 1215 is dedicated to him. ◆ ◆ ◆

Four years later he moved to New York and joined his brother Theodore at the George A. Fuller Construction Company as superintendent and assistant manager. In 1899 Goldwin and Theodore and their brothers Ralph and William formed their own company with Henry S. Thompson, the Thompson-Starrett Co. The brothers built the Algonquin between April and November 1902. It was Goldwin's first major project in Manhattan.

Goldwin Starrett next took an engineering position with the E. B. Ellis Granite Company in Vermont, which supplied the stone for many important New York structures, including the Woolworth Building. A few years later, he returned to New York and formed an architectural firm with Ernest Van Vleck, their office on the twenty-first floor of **8 West 40th Street.** Among the still-standing landmark buildings designed by Goldwin Starrett are:

- 1908: **200 Park Avenue South,** the high-rise **Everett Building**

- 1911: **609 Broad Street, Newark,** the **Hahne & Co.** department store

- 1914: **424 Fifth Avenue,** the flagship **Lord & Taylor** store

- 1916: **475 Tenth Avenue,** the fourteen-story white terra-cotta **Hill Publishing Building**

- 1916: **820 Fifth Avenue,** a thirteen-story luxury apartment house (in 2009, one apartment there sold for $40 million)

On May 9, 1918, Starrett died of pneumonia at his home in Glen Ridge, New Jersey. He was forty-three years old. Two of his brothers went on to build the Empire State Building.

The hotel had a colorful history long before the Vicious Circle showed up. It almost burned down twice in as many years: In February 1909, fire broke out in the restaurant and forced more than 350 guests out into the cold in their nightclothes. In November 1910, a more serious blaze occurred next door. Smoke poured into the Algonquin, 250 guests had to flee, and the "annex" was severely damaged inside. Thankfully, nobody was seriously injured.

Almost from the day it opened, the hotel has maintained close ties to the acting community. In 1905, twenty-six-year-old Ethel Barrymore had a suite, and her brothers, John and Lionel, often visited her sitting room. Their uncle John Drew lived in the hotel for seventeen years. Douglas Fairbanks and Mary Pickford frequently stayed here when not in Hollywood. Elsie Janis, Gertrude Lawrence, and Beatrice Lillie were just three of the many popular actresses who were guests during this era.

In 1911, Irish dramatist Lady Augusta Gregory was the first woman to smoke in the lobby—much to Frank Case's displeasure. However, Case didn't hesitate to promote the presence of celebrity guests to drum up business. In 1914, he took out an ad in the *Indianapolis Star* headed: "A few of the experienced travelers whose permanent New York home is the Hotel Algonquin," listing Broadway stars alongside Irvin S. Cobb, DeWolf Hopper, and the bishop of Kansas. In 1918, sixteen-year-old Tallulah Bankhead and her adult guardian took a room with a bath for $21 a week. Case told her family that he could look after the Algonquin or look after their daughter, but he couldn't do both.

During the Twenties, newspaper columnists mentioned the hotel practically every day. Broadway and vaudeville actors dined in the restaurant, and silent-film stars passed through the lobby. Visiting authors took up residence, including Gertrude Stein and H. L. Mencken. Sinclair Lewis was a frequent guest. One night in the

Oak Room, Lewis was eating a hamburger when a young woman approached his table and asked if he was Sinclair Lewis. Lewis replied: "No, but I happen to be his cousin. We do look very much alike, and the resemblance has proved very embarrassing to me. I happen to be a church worker, and some of my cousin's writings have offended me. *Elmer Gantry* in particular."

"I'm so pleased to hear you say that," said the woman, "because I feel the same way about him."

The Smiths employed Frank Case as the hotel's first general manager, and he built up the business. In May 1927, he bought the hotel from the Smiths for a little more than $717,000 (about $9.4 million today). The *New York Times* reported news of the sale on the front page, above the fold. He would own the business for another nineteen years.

Case became a celebrity while owning the hotel, and enjoyed rubbing shoulders with actors and writers who frequented the place. Mencken called Case "a somewhat dressy and vain fellow, and as he advanced in years he tried to conceal his age." But Case was a genius at marketing and advertising, and the hotel earned a national reputation.

After Case's death in 1946, his estate sold the Algonquin for about $1 million to Ben and Mary Bodne of Charleston, South Carolina. They had visited the hotel on their honeymoon in 1924 and had fallen in love with it. During World War II, Bodne made a fortune in the oil and coal business and moved his family to New York. The Bodnes bought a hotel that had seen better days: It had leaky pipes and worn-out furniture, and badly needed an overhaul. They immediately invested $300,000 in renovations. They dumped 300 beds, chairs, and tables and replaced them with exact replicas, even painting the walls the same colors. In the forty-one years that the Bodnes owned the Algonquin, the couple kept it in a state of

# Frank Case, Agreeable Hotelier

Frank Case became the most popular hotel owner in the nation and called the Algonquin home for forty-four years. He was born on November 27, 1871, in Buffalo. He worked locally as the night clerk at the Genesee Hotel before moving to Jersey City, New Jersey, in his twenties. There he managed the forty-year-old Taylor's Hotel. In 1897, he married Buffalo native Caroline Eckhart in a suite at Taylor's. Their daughter, Margaret, was born in 1902 as the Algonquin was being built. Case said that the couple couldn't afford a bassinet, so they put the baby in a hotel dresser drawer.

Frank Case, the hotel's first general manager, with actor Roy Atwell, right. ◆ ◆ ◆

Albert and Ann Foster, the Algonquin Hotel's first owners—who may have known Case in Buffalo—brought him on as manager. While the hotel was still under construction, he noticed that Goldwin Starrett had forgotten to include a restaurant and kitchen, thinking that all guests would eat out. Case changed the designs, and the planned gentlemen's billiards room became the hotel kitchen, where it remains today.

The couple had a son, Carroll, born in the hotel in 1908. Sadly, Caroline died four days later. Case raised the children in the hotel as a single parent with the help of hotel staff. After several years, Case married Bertha Walden, a hotel house-keeper who had traveled with actress Elsie Janis as a YMCA volunteer in France. The Case family lived in an apartment on the tenth floor. In early 1919, Frank and Bertha toured Belgium to advise on the construction of American-style hotels in the wake of the war. Later that year, with the Algonquin Round Table under way, Case saw the benefits of celebrity guests.

Case faced two business crises in his years in the hotel. First, he lost his taste for the lobby bar and the problems that came with heavy drinkers on the premises. He removed the bar from the hotel in 1917, three years ahead of Prohibition. No alcohol was served in the hotel for the next sixteen years. But for Case, a staff strike in 1939 spelled the end. The New York Hotel Trades Council of the American Federation of Labor backed the striking waiters. The staff walked out, and Case took it as a personal insult. He negotiated a contract with them, and the hotel has been a union shop ever since.

As Case got older and took up writing his memoirs, his love for the business waned. Case wrote three books about the Algonquin; all became popular. His health had declined by the end of World War II, and the Algonquin lost its first great hotelier.

Harpo Marx visits owners Ben and Mary Bodne in the Fifties. ◆ ◆ ◆

preservation. They retained anachronisms like elevator operators, and from the Fifties to the Eighties it was successful, becoming the family business. The couple's two daughters both married men who became Algonquin managers.

Writers and playwrights continued to patronize the hotel. William Faulkner wrote his Nobel Prize acceptance speech in his room in 1949. Six years later, Alan Jay Lerner and Frederick Loewe composed much of *My Fair Lady* in Suite 908; the racket they made shook the walls. Mary Chase, William Inge, and Arthur Miller all won the Pulitzer Prize for Drama, and all were guests. In 1959 filmmaker Preston Sturges came to a sad end in his suite. In the words of *The New Yorker*: "He died sad and gassy and alone, in the Algonquin Hotel, after too much coleslaw and beer." Two years later, James Thurber—blind, alcoholic, and alone—was carried out after a bad fall, dying a few weeks later.

During the Sixties, a new generation of writers became regulars, including John Cheever, Norman Mailer, William Saroyan, and Tennessee Williams. Brendan Behan was so pleased with his accommodations that he told the proprietor, "Mary, your son will live to be pope." She was Jewish and had two daughters. English actors came in droves, Sir Laurence Olivier, Joan Plowright, and Tony Richardson among them. European filmmakers also discovered the Algonquin's charms: Costa-Gavras, Jean-Luc Godard, Louis Malle, Eric Rohmer, and François Truffaut checked in. Vanessa Redgrave and Robert Shaw were followed by Yves Montand and Simone Signoret. (Mary Bodne babysat for Signoret.)

The hotel celebrated its seventy-fifth anniversary in October 1977 in high style. More than 250 guests attended a gala party hosted by *The New Yorker*. Editor William Shawn spied the crowd jammed between the front desk and the Rose Room and promptly left. Norman Mailer posed for photographers in the Blue Bar. Also in attendance were Mayor Abe Beame and former mayor John Lindsay. Writers were everywhere, including Ralph Ellison, Janet Flanner, Peter De Vries, and S. J. Perelman. Charles Addams delivered a gift: an illustration of Eustace Tilley blowing a bugle to salute the hotel, sporting a jagged scar on his chest. The only Round Table member in attendance was Marc Connelly. A reporter buttonholed the eighty-six-year-old and asked if the party conversation was as good as it was in the old days. Connelly smiled and said, "Mine is."

In 1987 the hotel changed hands for a fourth time when the Bodnes sold the hotel to the Aoki Corporation of Tokyo for $29 million. The couple remained in their tenth-floor apartment and each day sat in their favorite wingback chairs in the lobby. Ben died in 1991 at age eighty-eight, and Mary in 2003, at ninety-three. In the meantime, management company Caesar Park International sank more than $22 million into upgrading the hotel, three floors at a time, over the course of five years, also replacing the eighty-five-year-old elevators and all electrical systems.

In 1997, Aoki sold the hotel. A partnership between the Olympus Real Estate Corporation of Dallas and Camberley Hotels of Atlanta paid close to $33 million for the place. They, too, upgraded the hotel while maintaining its unique charm. They hired Alexandra Champalimaud, a Lisbon-born interior designer, to reimagine the lobby and make it appear more like it had in the past. They commissioned Brooklyn artist Natalie Ascencios to paint the core group of the Vicious Circle. The lobby—simultaneously new and old—took on a perpetual 5:30 p.m. happy-hour glow, where it was always the right time for a cocktail. One critic said, "The décor resembles an Italian monastery that's been turned into a five-star hotel." Business soared, and the occupancy rate increased.

The hotel celebrated its centennial with another change in ownership. In June 2002, Denver-based Miller Global Properties bought the hotel for $43 million. But after the sale a problem came to light: A previous owner believed the painting of the Round Table belonged to his company, not the hotel, and took it with him. That painting now hangs in the Martha Washington Hotel in Abingdon, Virginia. Miller scrambled to commission Ascencios to paint a new group portrait for the hundredth anniversary that fall.

In October 2002, the hotel marked the occasion in a low-key way. It had a cake-cutting ceremony in the Round Table Room (formerly the Rose Room) and unveiled a second beautiful painting. Management undertook another renovation, and for the first time in a hundred years the hotel was closed for a month. It reopened firmly in the new century with flat-screen televisions and wireless Internet access.

General manager Anthony Melchiorri ran a tight ship for Miller, embracing the hotel's history while making sure the business didn't coast on reputation alone. His attention to detail and savvy marketing helped to rejuvenate the hotel. Brooklyn-born Melchiorri launched one of the hotel's biggest publicity schemes: a $10,000 martini with a diamond engagement ring at the bottom of the glass. The story made international news. Miller owned the hotel for three and a half years, then sold it for a reported $74 million in late 2005 to HEI Hotels & Resorts, headquartered in Norwalk, Connecticut.

In May 2008, the new owners completed a $4.5 million renovation, installing new furnishings and amenities in all suites and guest rooms. Lobby changes included recessed lighting, pendant lights, and new furniture. Also in 2008, the owners hired Gary Budge as new general manager. He came with thirty-five years of industry experience at Sheraton and Starwood properties.

In 2010 the hotel entered another new era. The owners partnered with Marriott International, the hospitality company founded in 1927. The Algonquin became the first New York hotel to join the Autograph Collection, a small linked group of upscale global independent properties. These hotels and resorts fall into historic, boutique, or urban hotel categories. The Algonquin benefited from using Marriott's reservation system and affinity programs to market the hotel to new travelers.

HEI owned the Algonquin for a little more than five years. In June 2011, Cornerstone Real Estate Advisers of Hartford, Connecticut, bought the property for a little more than the previous sale price. A subsidiary of Massachusetts Mutual Life Insurance Company, Cornerstone made the most significant improvements to the hotel since the foundation was poured in 1902. Cornerstone shuttered the hotel and Blue Bar from January to May 2012, investing a reported $18 million in a top-to-bottom renovation that replaced all plumbing, electrical, and environmental systems in the building. Every room and suite were renovated and refurbished, with all carpets and wall decorations replaced. A new business center, fitness center, and guest hospitality area were added. Since the reopening the Algonquin has achieved Four Diamond recognition from the American Automobile Association.

In 2014 the hotel's first female general manager joined the team. Manuela "Manny" Rappenecker brought with her a quarter-century of experience managing hotels in Florida, New Jersey, and New York.

## 1. FRONT ENTRANCE AND FACADE

There is only one main entrance in the lobby on West 44th Street, making for a grander entrance into the lobby and increasing security because everyone must pass the front desk. The hotel has a Beaux Arts–inspired facade with continuous projecting metal bay windows and neo-Renaissance detail. The facade is executed in brick, with details in limestone, metal, and terra-cotta. The 1902 cornice has been removed, and the marquee has been replaced over the years. A cluster of bronze plaques on the front of the entrance attest to the hotel's prominence as a national literary landmark. New York City's Landmarks Preservation Commission granted the building landmark status in 1987, declaring that "the Algonquin Hotel has a special character, special historical and aesthetic interest and value as part of the development, heritage and cultural characteristics of New York City."

## 2. LOBBY

No space in the hotel has undergone more changes than the lobby. This is the heart and soul of the business, the gathering place for the public and guests alike. It has been renovated many times, most recently in 2012, when new lighting and custom furniture were installed. In 1902, the lobby had three businesses, all removed long ago: barbershop, newsstand, and bar. Guests haven't been able to get

INSIDE THE ALGONQUIN HOTEL

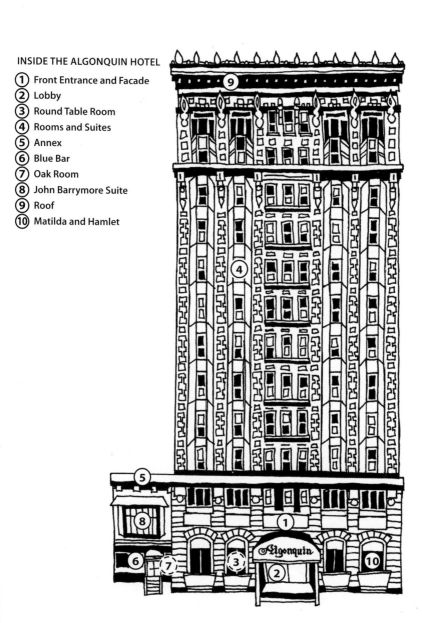

① Front Entrance and Facade
② Lobby
③ Round Table Room
④ Rooms and Suites
⑤ Annex
⑥ Blue Bar
⑦ Oak Room
⑧ John Barrymore Suite
⑨ Roof
⑩ Matilda and Hamlet

a hot shave since World War I. The bar was moved in 1991, and the newspaper vendor was packed off in 1998.

It's also a place of countless stories. Frank Case kicked Ruth Hale out of the lobby for smoking. In 1952, Audrey Hepburn, Elia Kazan, and Vivien Leigh received theater accolades here. Two decades later, Norman Mailer unveiled his book *Marilyn* to the press. During the 1977 New York City blackout, candles lit the lobby, and affable owner Ben Bodne served drinks on the house. Look for the beautiful grandfather clock, as old as the hotel and hand-wound daily. The intricate mosaic tile floor may look vintage, but it isn't. It was installed during a $5.5 million renovation in 1998.

## 3. ROUND TABLE ROOM

Seating for the hotel's main restaurant is located in the Round Table Room. Until 1998 it was called the Rose Room. When the

The painting by Natalie Ascencios adds to the glamour of the Round Table Room. ◆ ◆ ◆

group met here, Case moved them from the Pergola Room to the Rose Room and provided them with a large round table that could accommodate fifteen people. Where did the table go? Some believe it's one of the anonymous round tables in the Oak Room; others say it was lost in the Thirties. The current table is round and seats eight. The Ascencios painting of the Vicious Circle hangs where a bar once stood. When William Shawn was editor of *The New Yorker*, he had lunch (cornflakes) almost every day at a small table nearby. When he was forced out during a regime change, he attempted to run the magazine from the restaurant.

## 4. ROOMS AND SUITES

The most important feature in any hotel is the guest rooms. In 1902, that meant providing a clean bed and amenities such as a telephone and bath. The twenty-first-century guest desires wireless Internet access and allergy-free pillows. Because the hotel was built in 1902, many of the guest rooms are modest in size, but they have every modern convenience, and many have a story to tell. In 1924, in Suite 1105, Marc Connelly wrote the banquet scene for *To the Ladies* in three hours. According to Case, "The scene was played as he wrote it, without change."

All twenty-five of the suites carry names, including F.P.A (1112), Benchley (506), Parker (1106), and Ross (610). One of the more interesting is Suite 1010. For almost a hundred years, it was the owner's apartment. Frank Case lived here for more than forty-five years and raised a family in it. His son, Carroll, was born in the room in 1908. Case entertained countless friends here, including John Barrymore, John Drew, and Douglas Fairbanks. The next owners, Ben and Mary Bodne, moved into the suite in 1947. Mary lived there until 2000. Today 1010 is the Noël Coward Suite.

For many years, the New York Drama Critics' Circle voted for the best plays of the year in Suite 306, a tradition that began in 1935. Robert Benchley was among the nine original critics, and Case provided them with free liquor. Today 306 is the Edna Ferber Suite.

Following the 2012 renovation, the hotel today has 156 deluxe king and queen rooms. All have custom-made furniture and gadgets galore.

## 5. ANNEX

If you like sipping cocktails in the Blue Bar, you're standing in the same spot that horses and coachmen once stood after the Civil War. The bar is located in an annex—not part of the 1902 construction—attached to the hotel, formerly 65 West 44th Street. The Annex contains the bar and Oak Room on the first floor, the John Barrymore Suite and fitness center on the second floor, and hotel offices on the third. But in the nineteenth century, numerous stables for stage-coach lines lined 44th Street. The Annex is the last remaining carriage house on the block.

The hotel acquired the two-story stable in 1904 and added a third story the following year. The first floor was converted to a restaurant, and apartments were built above it. In 1910, a fire damaged the building. Second-floor resident Frederick Thompson, who developed Coney Island and built the Hippodrome Theatre, narrowly escaped the blaze. Beginning in 1911, the Rocky Mountain Club, a gentlemen's club for natives of Western states, leased the second and third floors for a clubhouse. The hotel used the first floor as the Pergola Room restaurant, the original meeting place of the Round Table. Later the third floor became a small ballroom for which Case booked orchestras to perform, among them Paul Whiteman. Case danced the turkey trot with notables such as Diamond Jim Brady and Florenz Ziegfeld. The hotel has renovated the Annex several times over the decades. For many years, the second floor was used for storage, until the 2012 renovation project carved out the John Barrymore Suite.

## 6. Blue Bar

The history of having mixed drinks in the Algonquin Hotel is a tale worthy of a double shot of brandy. In 1902 the bar was in the lobby, a stand-up operation without chairs. Gentlemen were welcome, but ladies couldn't enter by themselves. Cigars and cigarettes were permitted, and brass spittoons lined the room. On St. Patrick's Day, 1917, Case closed the bar well ahead of the Eighteenth Amendment. He claimed it was because his son was growing up in the hotel. "I have decided that I don't want to pay his school bills and the other costs

The Blue Bar circa 1935, when it was off the lobby. ◆ ◆ ◆

of bringing him up on the profits from booze," he told reporters. "I am not a prohibitionist nor a temperance missionary. . . . I don't want to be a rum seller." He kept the bar closed for sixteen years. When it reopened—in what is today the back of the restaurant—it was given a special touch. John Barrymore told Case that all actors look good in blue light, so recessed lighting was installed with blue gels.

The bar today, on the first floor of the Annex. ◆ ◆ ◆

The tradition stuck. The elegant corner bar thrived, but it didn't last long. For forty years, starting after World War II, it was a tiny wood-paneled nook near the front desk that the *Times* termed "claustrophobically romantic." When Hubert Humphrey was running for president, he ducked in for a double Canadian Club. In 1975, Lou Reed held court in sunglasses and scarf. That room was vacated in 1982 and became a coat closet and storage space.

The Blue Bar moved to its current location, the ground floor of the Annex, in 1997. It was decorated with prints of Al Hirschfeld drawings of Broadway stars. In 2006, the hotel held a ninetieth birthday party for bartender Hoy Wong, a beloved staff member since 1979. Some 350 people attended, and Mr. Hoy mixed martinis with ease. The Blue Bar went relatively untouched for twenty years until it closed in 2012 for five months of renovations. It reopened with the addition of tiny blue lights embedded in the extended and rebuilt bar, along with custom banquettes, polished oak walls, and decorative touches. The room increased in size, too, by about 20 percent.

## 7. OAK ROOM

For decades the Oak Room—another part of the Annex, and formerly the rear of the Pergola Room—was a formal dining room with tables and banquettes, and the location of the first meeting of the Vicious Circle in June 1919. The group adopted other nicknames for themselves, such as the Luigi Board, for their favorite waiter. Here Dorothy Parker had a memorable lunch with Scott and Zelda Fitzgerald. The trio sat in a line, their backs to the wall, at a long table. Parker remarked, "This looks like a road company of the Last Supper."

# A Policy of Kindness at the Front Desk

After World War II, when Ben and Mary Bodne owned the hotel, many notable black guests felt welcome in the hotel at a time when other hotels didn't accept their business. The Bodnes—Jews in the Jim Crow South—had experienced prejudice firsthand. Among the black celebrities who stayed at the hotel in the late Forties and early Fifties were jazz greats Ella Fitzgerald and Oscar Peterson. Celebrated contralto Marian Anderson was already a longtime visitor to the Algonquin when she became the first black singer at the Metropolitan Opera in 1955. Paul Robeson—a superstar in the Twenties after appearing in *Show Boat*—was also an Algonquin regular. The hotel welcomed civil rights activist Roy Wilkins, who led the National Association for the Advancement of Colored People in the Sixties. Maya Angelou was also an Algonquin guest in the early Seventies.

The room was repurposed as a cabaret in 1981. Among the stars to launch their careers here were Harry Connick Jr. and Diana Krall. The room has theatrical lighting, sound equipment, and a grand piano. Today it's used for special events.

### 8. JOHN BARRYMORE SUITE

The hotel had a special relationship with John Barrymore for more than forty years. Born John Sidney Blyth in Philadelphia in 1882, Barrymore first came to the hotel in his twenties. To hotel staff, he was a beloved rake and raconteur, and no actor touched Frank Case's heart more than Barrymore. In public the actor wore old clothes and sloppy hats, and when he ran out of clean shirts, he borrowed ill-fitting ones from Case.

John Barrymore and his second wife, Michael Strange, in 1922. ◆ ◆ ◆

Onstage, Barrymore was notorious for changing his lines. At one matinée he spied Case in the audience and reworked his dialogue to say he'd pay his bill when he got around to it. When the hotel was renovated in 2012, a large new luxury suite was carved out of the second floor of the Annex, directly above the Blue Bar. Suite 209, the John Barrymore Suite, features two levels, a dressing room, and a bathroom bigger than some New York apartments. It is the largest room in the hotel, at 700 square feet. One reviewer

The John Barrymore Suite today. ◆ ◆ ◆

called it "the greatest hotel room in New York." Barrymore would appreciate that it's the suite closest to the Blue Bar.

## 9. ROOF

The hotel's roof is no longer open to the public. In the early days, Case had a roof garden and patio for guests in the era before air-conditioning made New York summers tolerable. Case once tried sleeping under the stars—hauling a New York City park bench to the roof and sleeping on it for two

Margaret Case grew up in the hotel and played on its roof. As an adult, she wrote for *The New Yorker*. ◆ ◆ ◆

nights—with dismal results. Longtime resident Douglas Fairbanks Sr. used the roof as an outdoor gymnasium and personal playground for exercising and rehearsal. Case's young daughter, Margaret, often went up to the roof to skip rope with the legendary actor. The two climbed around on the fire escapes and once climbed into the cornice and got stuck.

### 10. Matilda and Hamlet

The hotel's resident cat, Matilda, a purebred Ragdoll, is a fixture in the lobby and pampered like a VIP. The tradition of keeping a cat in the lobby goes back at least to the Thirties, when John Barrymore was a guest. Case took in a stray he named Rusty, but according to popular legend, Barrymore told Case that because he ran a theatrical and literary hotel, the cat should be named Hamlet. To this day, any male carries that name, and females are Matilda. (Why Matilda, nobody knows.)

One of the most spoiled felines in the city. ◆ ◆ ◆

Bellmen look after Matilda, and her favorite lobby spot is on top of a luggage cart or behind the (warm) computer monitor on the front desk. In 2001, Matilda appeared in the children's book *The Algonquin Cat* by Val Schaffner, illustrated by Hilary Knight, who also illustrated the Eloise series. Matilda also appears in *The Vicious Circle* painting in the Round Table Room. The hotel hosts a summertime birthday gala for the cat, raising thousands of dollars for animal charity groups.

# {4}
# INK-STAINED WRETCHES
## Newspapers and Journalists

*It seems to me not unfair to say that America leads the world in hypocrisy, and always has, despite the sharpest kind of competition from Great Britain.*

—HEYWOOD BROUN

In the Twenties, New York City had more than fifteen daily newspapers. Many people read both a morning paper and then an evening edition after work. The Round Table actively participated in the world of journalism, its members ranking among the most widely read writers of their era. Their king, of course, was Franklin P. Adams, followed closely by Heywood Broun and Alexander Woollcott. Other newspaper wage slaves were Robert Benchley—who happily flunked out of daily journalism—Marc Connelly, Jane Grant, Ruth Hale, George S. Kaufman, Herman Mankiewicz, William Murray, Laurence Stallings, Frank Sullivan, Deems Taylor, and John V. A. Weaver. The Round Table got its start because of a newspaper critic (Woollcott), and the group's fame grew largely due to the columnists at the table who wrote about their lunch companions.

Before the rise of radio and television, all of the major newspapers had offices on Newspaper Row at the intersection of Park Row and Nassau and Spruce Streets. Lined up like battleships were

The spire of the Tribune Building before it was demolished in 1966. ◆ ◆ ◆

Newspaper Row, circa 1905, from left: the *World*, the *Sun* (smaller building in foreground), the *Tribune*, the *Times*. Only the *Times* building, now Pace University, still stands today. ◆ ◆ ◆

the offices of the *World*, *Sun*, *Tribune*, and *Times*, all in beautiful stone edifices designed by the best architects of the day. This city within a city was the center of the media universe before World War I. The newsmen had their own saloons, restaurants, and cafés. When the subway opened in 1904, the first entrance went in across the street, at City Hall. The intersection of Park Row and Spruce Street, now Pace Plaza, once was known as Printing House Square. Newspaper Row was demolished beginning in the Fifties. Today Pace University occupies most of the area where the newspapers were published.

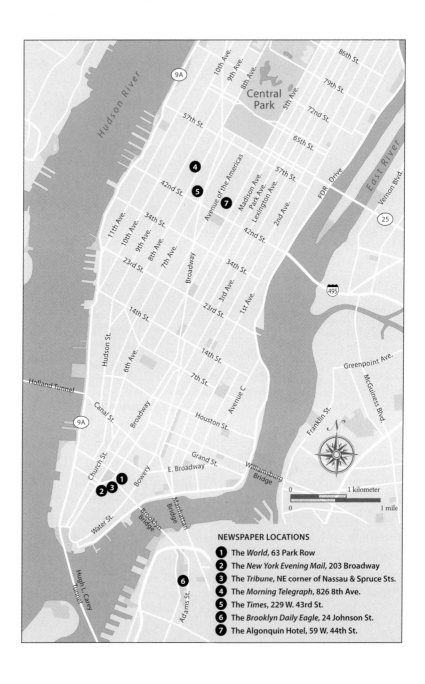

**NEWSPAPER LOCATIONS**

1. The *World*, 63 Park Row
2. The *New York Evening Mail*, 203 Broadway
3. The *Tribune*, NE corner of Nassau & Spruce Sts.
4. The *Morning Telegraph*, 826 8th Ave.
5. The *Times*, 229 W. 43rd St.
6. The *Brooklyn Daily Eagle*, 24 Johnson St.
7. The *Algonquin Hotel*, 59 W. 44th St.

## 1. THE *WORLD*

Since the Colonial era, scores of papers have come and gone in New York City, but none was more lamented than the *New York World*. The paper played an important part in American history, and its impact still resonates. Founded in 1860, it lost money until 1883, when Hungarian immigrant Joseph Pulitzer bought it for $240,000 from financier Jay Gould.

There were three separate editions and staffs: morning, evening, and Sunday. Depending on the perspective, Pulitzer either stands tallest in American journalism history, or he's seen as a massive egoist, putting anything into the *World* to draw readers. He helmed an empire that engaged readers and took an active part in their lives. (His newspaper delivery vans handed out bread to the poor, inventing the bread line.) The *World* was as well known for its philanthropic work as it was for publishing pieces by Mark Twain and O. Henry. The editorial page supported a fund-raising campaign for the pedestal on which the Statue of Liberty stands.

The *World* stood at **63 Park Row,** with editorial offices on the eleventh floor of a tower that Pulitzer erected in 1890. A golden dome topped the 309-foot-tall building. Pulitzer died in 1911, and the paper ran for twenty more years.

Star reporter Herbert Bayard Swope became executive editor in 1921 and brought in the best talent, increasing high-quality reporting and also hiring New York's first black reporter. By the time the Round Table came to it, the highly respected *World* was the "newspaperman's newspaper." Swope receives credit for creating the page opposite the editorial page—the "Op. Ed."—a phrase he coined. Onto this page he brought a lively mix of writers, most from the Vicious Circle. Among the first of them to write for the *World* was Robert Benchley, a month after he quit *Vanity Fair* in 1920. Benchley's book

The only known remaining piece of the Pulitzer Building is this stained-glass window, now in the World Room at the Columbia School of Journalism. The Pulitzer Prize committee meets in this room. ◆ ◆ ◆

reviews often had nothing to do with the books themselves, and could easily contain ruminations on train schedules.

Swope poached Broun and Adams from the *Tribune* in 1921. The thirty-three-year-old Broun could write anything, from a play review to a recap of the Harvard–Yale football game. He had free rein in his column "It Seems to Me," which ran for six years, to discuss books, sports, movies, or politics. The last of these landed him in hot water when Broun butted heads with Swope. When F.P.A. brought his famous "Conning Tower" to the op-ed page, it caused a sensation.

Dorothy Parker was a regular contributor; F.P.A. and the *World* published her two best-known poems, "Résumé" and "News Item," on the same day in 1925. F.P.A. also gave big breaks to James Thurber and E. B. White, who landed on *The New Yorker* together a few years later. Swope hired Deems Taylor as music critic at a time when it was unheard of to hire a composer for that role. But Taylor, warmly received and much praised, set the standard for thoughtful music criticism. He lasted four years on the staff.

Laurence Stallings joined in 1922 to write book reviews and editorials. The passionately liberal war veteran referred to a black man as "Mr." in print, angering readers in his Georgia hometown. The other veteran to join the *World* that year was Herman Mankiewicz, who came straight from working in Berlin. A native New Yorker, Mankiewicz had grown up with the paper.

In 1923 Woollcott left the *Times* for the *World* to be lead drama critic. He received $15,000 a year and three months' vacation. The other great talent on the staff was humorist Frank Sullivan, who joined at the same time. When F.P.A. went on vacation, Sullivan filled his "Conning Tower" column and was such a hit that he was taken off straight reporting. Sullivan was so distraught when the Pulitzer brothers sold the newspaper in 1931, throwing three thousand men and women out of work, that he quit the newspaper business and moved back home to Saratoga Springs.

## Journalism

*Journalism's a shrew and a scold;*
*I like her.*
*She makes you sick, she makes you old;*
*I like her.*
*She's daily trouble, scorn, and strife;*
*She's love and hate and death and life;*
*She ain't no lady—she's my wife;*
*I like her.*
     —Franklin P. Adams in the *World*,
          February 27, 1931

Today no plaque or monument marks the former Pulitzer Building and its wonderful gold dome. Before it was razed in 1955, Swope and F.P.A. toured the deserted newsroom one last time. It's now a highway approach to the Brooklyn Bridge. The stained-glass window from the city room was moved to Columbia University's Journalism School building, where, each year in the World Room, the Pulitzer Prize winners are announced.

## 2. THE *NEW YORK EVENING MAIL*

The *Evening Mail* made Franklin P. Adams a celebrity in New York. His column "Always in Good Humor" began on the editorial page in 1904; later he changed the title to "The Conning Tower." Among his hundreds of contributors were Edna Ferber, Ring Lardner, Sinclair Lewis, Edna St. Vincent Millay, Alice Duer Miller, and Dorothy Parker. Almost six years after arriving in New York, F.P.A. achieved national fame for a dashed-off piece of verse. On the occasion of a trip to the Polo Grounds, the home ballpark of the New York Giants, Adams watched his beloved Chicago Cubs fail. Returning to work— in the days when all baseball games took place in the afternoon—F.P.A. turned into the composing room

The *Evening Mail* building, on the right, in 1908. The Singer Tower, under construction, is next door on Broadway. Both have been demolished. ◆ ◆ ◆

"Baseball's Sad Lexicon" about Cubs infielders Joe Tinker, Johnny Evers, and Frank Chance. All three went into the National Baseball Hall of Fame together, due in large part to F.P.A.'s immortal words of July 10, 1910:

> *These are the saddest of possible words:*
> *"Tinker to Evers to Chance,"*
> *Trio of bear cubs, and fleeter than birds,*
> *Tinker and Evers and Chance.*
> *Ruthlessly pricking our gonfalon bubble,*
> *Making a Giant hit into a double—*
> *Words that are heavy with nothing but trouble:*
> *"Tinker to Evers to Chance."*

## Baseball and Broadway

One day in 1915, Heywood Broun learned that he was being moved from the *Tribune* sports department to the drama desk. In the late morning, he took the subway to the Polo Grounds and covered the Giants game, serving as official scorer. One of the players felt the scoring was subpar and told the manager. In the evening, Broun had an aisle seat to review Ethel Barrymore's new play at the Lyceum Theatre. He panned her performance. The next day the *Trib*'s managing editor received two angry letters. The first, from the Giants front office, demanded: "What's the idea of sending a drama critic to cover a ball game?" The other, from Barrymore: "How dare you send a cheap baseball writer to review a play opening?"

When F.P.A. quit the *Evening Mail* in 1914 to go to the *Tribune*, his handpicked successor was one of his favorite contributors: George S. Kaufman. The younger man had been sending pieces to F.P.A. since 1908, and his mentor recommended him for the job. Another future Round Tabler whom F.P.A. helped get a job on the *Evening Mail* was Brock Pemberton, who arrived in New York from Kansas with a suitcase and little else. Both Kaufman and Pemberton started their New York careers on the *Evening Mail*. Another friend of the group was esteemed sports scribe Grantland Rice.

The *New York Evening Mail* was located at **203 Broadway,** a few blocks south of Newspaper Row, across the street from St. Paul's Chapel. In January 1924, the *Evening Mail* ceased to exist after it was bought and merged into the *Telegram*. Today the building is an office tower.

### 3. The *New-York Tribune*

Heywood Broun joined the *Tribune* around 1912 at a salary of $25 a week. He was a general assignment reporter before being put on the sports desk. His first assignment was to interview pitcher Christy Mathewson of the Giants. Broun beat him at checkers instead and later became the future Cooperstown legend's bridge partner. When the Giants went to the 1912 World Series, Broun covered the game for the *Tribune*. Broun was among the first reporters to earn a byline, not often given out then.

Franklin P. Adams, who wrote pieces for the *Trib*'s Sunday magazine in 1906, was lured away from the *Evening Mail* in 1914 with the amazing salary of $25,000 a year (about $595,000 today). He and Broun became fast friends in the city room. Within a year, F.P.A. brought over his protégé, Kaufman, who started out covering the shipping news and later moved to the drama department. The future playwright soaked up the Broadway world, putting what he learned into his writing.

The *Tribune* merged with the *Herald* in 1924 and moved uptown to **225 West 40th Street.** Publication of the *New York Herald Tribune* collapsed in 1966 amid a labor strike. The Tribune Building, once the tallest in Manhattan, was at **150 Nassau Street** on Newspaper Row. It was a beautiful Neo-Grecian tower designed in 1873 by Richard Morris Hunt, who also designed the Fifth Avenue facade of the Metropolitan Museum of Art. The Tribune Building was demolished in 1966.

## 4. The *Morning Telegraph*

No paper in New York had a reputation quite like the *Morning Telegraph*, which ran from 1840 to 1972. If you read it, you wanted news of horse racing, vaudeville, and Broadway gossip. It was the kind of place that let chorus girls hang around the newsroom after they got off work. The sports editor in the Twenties was the Old West gunslinger Bat Masterson. Reporter John J. Fitz Gerald popularized the nickname "Big Apple" for New York City while on the paper.

The *Morning Telegraph* perfectly fit Broun and Connelly. Broun's career at the *Morning Telegraph* started with an internship at the paper, arranged by his father, the summer following his sophomore year at Harvard. After the fiasco of flunking French and not earning his diploma in 1910, Broun was hired full-time. At age twenty-two, he was covering baseball games, interviewing actresses, and writing editorials—sometimes all in the same day—while making $25 a week and loving it. When he found out that book critics got free review copies, he started writing a literary column. When he asked for a raise and byline two years later, he was shown the door.

Connelly had an easier time when he joined during World War I; at least he was a real reporter. Connelly, a leg man in Pittsburgh, had come to New York with a play he'd written. When that didn't pan out, he went looking for a journalism job. "In 1917 and 1918 the *Morning Telegraph* printed so much theatrical news that it was known as the chorus girl's breakfast," he recalled years later. While covering show business, Connelly met his first collaborator, Kaufman, who had the same beat for the *Times*.

The paper, published for 132 years, ceased publication during a printers' union strike in 1972. The *Morning Telegraph* offices were at **826 Eighth Avenue.** The building has since been demolished.

### 5. THE *NEW YORK TIMES*

No newspaper looms over American culture today more than the *New York Times*. But that wasn't the case in the era of silent films, speakeasies, and flappers. In the Jazz Age, the *World* and the *Tribune* had the reputation for good writing and reporting. The *Times* was just one of a dozen newspapers in the crowded New York news market, but it prevailed by means of superior editing and wise business decisions. The *Times* always had strong publishers, while the others changed hands and suffered from poor management.

The *Times* began in 1851 at **113 Nassau Street** with Henry J. Raymond as editor. The paper wasn't very successful, but its fortunes improved in 1896 when it began a new era under publisher Adolph S. Ochs. His descendants have run the paper for more than a century. In 1857, the *Times* occupied a building at **41 Park Row.** Just eight years after Ochs took over the paper, the *Times* moved to Longacre Square, renamed Times Square in 1904. The *Times* outgrew the building in a few short years, and in 1913 it moved to the home it would occupy for more than ninety years, located at **229 West 43rd Street.**

The *Times* occupied this landmark building from 1913 to 2007. ◆ ◆ ◆

Around this time the first future Round Table member joined the staff. Alexander Woollcott was twenty-two years old in 1909. The recent Hamilton grad went to work on the city desk. His most harrowing assignment was being sent to Nova Scotia to report on the dead from the RMS *Titanic* in April 1912. Soon after, he moved to the drama department, where he remained for almost twenty years as the city's preeminent theater critic.

Next to join the staff was Jane Grant, who unwittingly became the first female general assignment reporter on the *Times*. She started out answering the phones in the society department and moved up to covering hotels and weddings. Her quick thinking and verve got her promoted shortly after World War I. She interviewed Charlie Chaplin in 1921 ("Circumstances made a comedian of him and he has given the best in him to a laughter-loving world," she wrote). In 1934 she went to Tokyo to interview Emperor Hirohito of Japan, then traveled to Berlin several weeks later to meet the Nazi government. In 1935 she was the first woman from the *Times* to report from Moscow.

# The Ball and the Building

On December 31, 1904, the *New York Times* celebrated its move from Newspaper Row into a twenty-five-story building called the Times Tower on the northwest corner of 42nd Street and Broadway. Fireworks were set off, and Longacre Square became Times Square. Cyrus Eidlitz and Andrew McKenzie designed the tall, narrow building that hosted the paper for fewer than ten years, when the offices moved one block north to West 43rd Street. Later, the Renaissance-style terracotta was stripped off, and enormous billboards, called "spectaculars" in New York City, were attached to its sides. In 1907 the city banned fireworks in Times Square, so publisher Adolph S. Ochs asked that a 700-pound wooden ball with one hundred lightbulbs be lowered to usher in 1908. For more than a hundred years, millions of spectators have watched the ball lowered on its roof on New Year's Eve.

George S. Kaufman joined the drama department and worked under Woollcott. Even when Kaufman became a hit maker, he kept his day job for a number of years, fearful that his playwriting spell might stop. Others who wrote freelance pieces for the *Times* included Ruth Hale, Dorothy Parker, and Laurence Stallings. In 2007, the staff moved into a new office tower at **620 Eighth Avenue.** The old offices were converted to retail shops, restaurants, and offices. A bowling alley now occupies the former editorial offices.

## 6. The *Brooklyn Daily Eagle*

The *Brooklyn Daily Eagle* was in its time one of the most-read newspapers in the country. With offices at the **corner of Johnson and Washington,** it was founded by Isaac Van Anden in October 1842 and was like a *Times* for Brooklynites. Walt Whitman was editor from 1846 to 1848, and another editor, Henry C. Murphy, was the state senator instrumental in building the Brooklyn Bridge. In 1897, editor in chief St. Clair McKelway opposed Brooklyn consolidation with the other four boroughs to make up greater New York City— futilely, as it turned out.

The *Eagle*, a vital newspaper, attracted talented writers and editors to its staff. Among them was John V. A. Weaver, who came to New York and befriended Woollcott. Through Woollcott, Weaver met William B. Murray, music critic for the *Eagle*. Weaver became literary editor. Ruth Hale contributed, too; when she wasn't ghost-writing book reviews for her husband, Heywood Broun, she wrote about them for the *Eagle*.

The *Eagle* folded in 1955. In 1996, a new weekday publication launched under the old name.

One of Heywood Broun's many projects was writing, producing, and starring in a 1931 Broadway revue called *Shoot the Works* at George M. Cohan's Theatre, formerly at 1482 Broadway. It lasted for ninety performances. In the front row is Connie Madison, whom Broun married in 1935. ◆ ◆ ◆

# {5}

# RAISING THE CURTAIN

## Broadway's Golden Age and Its Round Table Stars

*When I was born I owed twelve dollars.*
—GEORGE S. KAUFMAN

The single unifying element among almost all members of the Round Table was the live theater business. Sitting at the table at any given point was at least one person who made his or her living on Broadway. Some wrote the shows that others acted, while across the table critics lay in wait to tear both of them down. Press agents drummed up publicity and ticket sales, so they sat next to the newspaper columnist who needed backstage gossip for the next day's edition. Directors and producers, the men behind the scenes, were among the most powerful in the city. Young actresses floated into the hotel dining room and held their own at the table. All bonded over grilled chicken and potatoes on West 44th Street.

Broadway was vastly different in 1920 from what it has become today. Audiences then were considerably larger; live theater had no competition from radio and television. Motion pictures were still silent, and their impact was just beginning to register. The simplest figure to know is the number of Broadway playhouses in operation then: 76 "legitimate" theaters. In 2014, the number was 40. Other stats: The average number of plays (dramas, musical comedies, revues, and operettas) produced annually on Broadway in 1920 was

225. In 1927, the peak year for live theater in the decade, 268. In the 2012–13 season: just 46 new productions. In the Twenties, sometimes as many as five new shows opened on the same night.

The Theater District was the Vicious Circle's stomping ground. Within ten blocks lay the supper clubs, speakeasies, hotels, and some of the newspapers. After World War II, the theater business contracted. Many venerable stages became movie theaters, and some ended life showing X-rated films in the Sixties and Seventies. As real estate values rose, the buildings fell to the wrecking ball. Today, the former locations of scores of theaters have become office buildings and hotels.

### I. THE CORT

Built by West Coast theater owner John Cort and designed by Thomas W. Lamb in the style of the Petit Trianon at Versailles, the 1,084-seat Cort opened in December 1912. *Merton of the Movies*—one of the biggest hits for the Kaufman and Connelly team—played there for 392 performances, from November 1922 to October 1923. Kaufman famously cracked, "Satire on the stage is what closes on Saturday night,"

The Cort is the only surviving, still active, legitimate theater designed by Thomas W. Lamb. ◆ ◆ ◆

but the show, a satire about a shy, movie-mad grocery clerk who goes to Hollywood and becomes a silent-film star because he is such a terrible actor, was a smash. In 1987, the New York City Landmarks

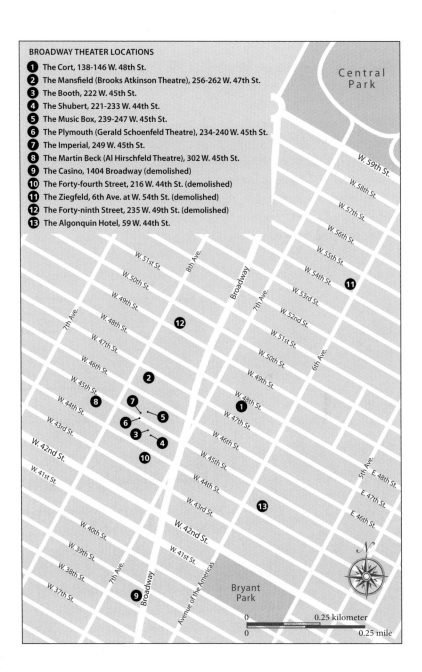

BROADWAY THEATER LOCATIONS

1. The Cort, 138-146 W. 48th St.
2. The Mansfield (Brooks Atkinson Theatre), 256-262 W. 47th St.
3. The Booth, 222 W. 45th St.
4. The Shubert, 221-233 W. 44th St.
5. The Music Box, 239-247 W. 45th St.
6. The Plymouth (Gerald Schoenfeld Theatre), 234-240 W. 45th St.
7. The Imperial, 249 W. 45th St.
8. The Martin Beck (Al Hirschfeld Theatre), 302 W. 45th St.
9. The Casino, 1404 Broadway (demolished)
10. The Forty-fourth Street, 216 W. 44th St. (demolished)
11. The Ziegfeld, 6th Ave. at W. 54th St. (demolished)
12. The Forty-ninth Street, 235 W. 49th St. (demolished)
13. The Algonquin Hotel, 59 W. 44th St.

Preservation Commission designated the French neoclassical interior and exterior of the theater as landmarks.

## 2. Mansfield Theatre (Brooks Atkinson Theatre)

The 1,044-seat theater was originally named for nineteenth-century actor Richard Mansfield. Herbert J. Krapp, architect on half a dozen other theaters from the era, designed it in 1926. It has a striking interior, due in part to one of the interior designers having been the former architect to Czar Nicholas II.

Marc Connelly won his only Pulitzer Prize for *The Green Pastures*, which played at the Mansfield for 640 performances in

Many members of the cast of *The Green Pastures* lived in Harlem. ◆ ◆ ◆

1930–31. Adapting a book by Roark Bradford of sketches and stories picked up from plantations in the Deep South, Connelly retold the Old Testament through the eyes of southern blacks with a large, all-black cast. Benchley, writing in *The New Yorker*, said: "I do not ever remember crying before over the thing that made me cry almost continuously as *The Green Pastures*. I cried because here was something so good. . . . You have never seen anything like *The Green Pastures* in the theater before, and you are not likely to see anything like it again, for it could not be imitated."

The theater was renamed in 1960 for the *Times* theater critic Brooks Atkinson.

## 3. Booth Theatre

The Booth is one of the oldest and most intimate theaters on Broadway. Named for actor Edwin Booth—brother of Lincoln assassin John Wilkes Booth—it opened in October 1913. Henry B. Herts, architect of the neighboring Shubert Theatre, designed it in the Italian Renaissance style. The 800-plus-seat Booth was built for drama and comedies and has a warm atmosphere. It also has an

Peggy Wood and Clifton Webb in *Blithe Spirit.* ◆ ◆ ◆

unusual feature: a wall between the auditorium and the entranceway to dampen street noise from West 45th Street.

George S. Kaufman approached Edna Ferber about adapting a 1922 short story she'd written, "Old Man Minick," about a tightly knit Chicago family. Ferber jumped at the chance, and the pair banged out a script for *Minick*, their first theater collaboration. "I didn't think there was a play in *Minick*, and I don't to this day," Ferber wrote afterward. When the play opened in September 1924, with Antoinette Perry as Lil Corey, reviews were good ... except in the *Times*: "Woollcott loosed vials of vitriol out of all proportion to the gentle little play's importance," she recounted. The play ran for 141 performances until January 1925. Although not a big success, it showed that Kaufman and Ferber could work together, which they did again.

Another Round Table member starred in a smash hit at the Booth. Noël Coward tapped Peggy Wood for the role of Ruth Condomine in *Blithe Spirit* when the play transferred from London to New York. The comedy ran for more than 650 performances between 1941 and 1943. The Booth attained city landmark protection in 1987.

## 4. Shubert Theatre

Named for producer Sam S. Shubert, killed in a 1905 Pennsylvania train wreck, the Shubert opened fourteen days before the Booth in October 1913. In time, Shubert's brothers, Lee and Jacob, built a theatrical empire that still stands today. Henry B. Herts designed the 1,400-seat Venetian Renaissance theater at the same time he worked on the Booth, and decorated the Shubert with elaborate plasterwork and murals.

The first play to win a Pulitzer Prize in the Shubert was Robert E. Sherwood's *Idiot's Delight* in 1936. An antiwar satire set in a hotel in fascist Italy on the eve of World War II, the show was a sensation, and ran for three hundred performances in 1936–37, starring

Sam Shubert, for whom the theater is named, died tragically. ◆ ◆ ◆

Alfred Lunt, Lynn Fontanne, and Sydney Greenstreet. Sherwood wrote later: "It was completely American in that it represented a compound of blank pessimism and desperate optimism, of chaos and jazz."

In 1996, the Shubert was restored to its former glory and its central ceiling mural re-created. In the lobby, look for the somber framed portrait of Sam S. Shubert, who died at age twenty-eight.

## 5. Music Box Theatre

Designed by C. Howard Crane and E. George Kiehler and built for Irving Berlin and producer Sam H. Harris, the Music Box Theatre opened in September 1922 with Irving Berlin's *Music Box Revue*. Moss Hart described it as everyone's dream of a theater.

In the Thirties, George S. Kaufman had a string of hits here. Kaufman and Morrie Ryskind's *Of Thee I Sing* was the first musical to win a Pulitzer Prize, and it happened here in 1931. With Edna Ferber, Kaufman collaborated on *Dinner at Eight* in 1932, which ran for 232 performances, and *Stage Door* in 1936, for 169 shows. But his biggest hit of all

The Music Box Theatre has four Federal Revival columns in front of what was once a smokers' porch. ◆ ◆ ◆

was based on his old boss, Alexander Woollcott. With Moss Hart, Kaufman cowrote *The Man Who Came to Dinner*, which opened in October 1939 and ran for 739 performances.

The Music Box was designated a city landmark in 1987.


## 6. The Plymouth Theatre (Gerald Schoenfeld Theatre)

Herbert J. Krapp, also the architect of the Longracre, designed the Plymouth in 1917, the patterned brickwork on the exterior its most significant architectural element.

Laurence Stallings and Maxwell Anderson were both working at the *New York World* when they decided to collaborate on a play. Stallings, who'd lost a leg in combat as a Marine, knew he wanted to write an antiwar drama. The pair cowrote *What Price Glory?* for producer-director Arthur Hopkins, the first play to use the profanity-laced speech of soldiers. Its grim view of war riveted audiences, and it was a hit at the Plymouth in September 1924, running for 433 performances and landing its playwrights Hollywood contracts.

Another of the many successful shows on the Plymouth stage was Robert E. Sherwood's 1939 Pulitzer Prize winner, *Abe Lincoln in Illinois*, with Raymond Massey as the sixteenth president.

This theater was declared a city landmark in 1987. After eighty-eight years as the Plymouth, it was renamed in 2005 for Gerald Schoenfeld, a lawyer and chairman of the Shubert Organization.


## 7. Imperial Theatre

The Imperial opened in 1923 as a musical comedy theater with a capacity of more than 1,600 seats, also designed by the Shubert brothers' go-to architect, Herbert J. Krapp.

Here George S. Kaufman had one of his rare flops. The 1933 musical *Let 'Em Eat Cake* was a sequel to *Of Thee I Sing*, the latter a hit in 1931. With lyrics by Ira Gershwin and music by George Gershwin, it had the same cast and characters as the previous show but was darker, and its Depression themes didn't win over audiences.

In 1987 the city gave landmark status to the interior but not the exterior.

## 8. Martin Beck Theatre (Al Hirschfeld Theatre)

Vaudeville mogul Martin Beck planned one of the grandest of all Broadway playhouses. He tapped noted San Francisco architect G. Albert Lansburgh to create a Moorish-inspired building with elaborate, Byzantine-style details. Painter Albert Herter embellished an

Arabian Nights theme so that theatergoers would forget they were sitting in Hell's Kitchen. Lansburgh, who later designed the El Capitan in Hollywood, built the playhouse like a movie palace. Beck wanted to attract musical spectacles, so he added dressing rooms to hold a cast of 200. Originally the theater had around 1,200 seats; today it seats more than 1,400.

Robert E. Sherwood wrote *Reunion in Vienna* for Alfred Lunt and Lynn

Lynn Fontanne as Elena and Alfred Lunt as Rudolph Maximilian von Hapsburg in *Reunion in Vienna.* ◆ ◆ ◆

Fontanne, and it became one of the biggest hits of his career, play-ing at the Martin Beck for 264 performances from 1931–32. But the most famous anecdote about the Martin Beck involves Dorothy Parker. The erstwhile drama critic attended *The Lake* in 1933, a flop that featured a twenty-six-year-old Katharine Hepburn. As the leg-end goes—because the tale doesn't appear in any published Parker reviews—a friend asked Parker what she thought of Hepburn's per-formance. "She ran the gamut of emotions—from A to B." The story got back to the actress, who years later admitted to making the sign of the cross whenever she passed the theater.

The Martin Beck received landmark status in 1987, its interior described as "unlike any other Broadway theater." It was renamed in 2003 for cartoonist Al Hirschfeld.

## 9. CASINO THEATRE
## (DEMOLISHED, 1930)

A beloved playhouse on the cor-ner of Broadway and 39th Street, the Moorish-influenced Casino opened in 1882 with about 900 seats. It was the first theater with a roof garden, the first lit entirely by electricity, and the first to feature a chorus line—the Florodora Girls in 1900.

In 1924, the Marx Brothers lit up Broadway in their first show, *I'll Say She Is*, at the Casino. Crit-

Four Horse (Laugh) Men of Broadway

Russell Henderson caricature from the *New York Evening Post*, July 1924. ◆ ◆ ◆

ics took notice. One of them was George S. Kaufman, who wanted to work with them. Their first collaboration was the Marx Brothers' second show, *The Cocoanuts*, with music and lyrics by Irving Berlin, which played at the Lyric Theatre for 276 performances and made huge stars of the brothers. Kaufman wrote the comedy based on a Florida real estate swindle and confidence men. Typical of Kaufman's humor was a scene with Groucho, Chico, and a map: Chico thinks that "levees" is the Jewish neighborhood; Groucho tells him "Well, we'll Passover that." Harpo stole scenes with his silence and even played some of Gershwin's *Rhapsody in Blue* on his harp. In 2014, *I'll Say She Is* was revived Off-Off-Broadway to mark the centennial of the brothers adopting their "-o" nicknames.

The Casino was demolished in 1930.

## 10. FORTY-FOURTH STREET THEATRE (DEMOLISHED, 1946)

The Forty-fourth Street Theatre opened in November 1912 as the Weber and Fields Music Hall, named by the Shuberts for the popular musical comedy team of the Gay Nineties. The duo had reunited after years of fighting, but two months after the theater was named in their honor, they split for good, so their names came off the building.

Shakespeare and musical comedies filled the nearly 1,500-seat house for thirty years. The Marx Brothers' biggest Broadway hit, *Animal Crackers*, opened here in 1928. During World War II the theater hosted the Stage Door Canteen, a popular destination for service members to meet Broadway and Hollywood stars. Among the backers were Round Tablers Brock Pemberton and Peggy Wood. The final show was Leonard Bernstein, Adolph Green, and Betty Comden's *On the Town* in 1945. The playhouse was demolished the next year to make way for an annex to the *New York Times* printing plant on 44th Street. Today a bowling alley, theme restaurants, and exhibition space stand in its place, but a bronze plaque marks the spot where the theater once stood.

The Ziegfeld once grandly occupied the corner of Sixth Avenue and 54th Street. ◆ ◆ ◆

## 11. Ziegfeld Theatre (demolished, 1966)

The Ziegfeld Theatre opened in January 1927. Will Rogers helped to dedicate the cornerstone for the playhouse, cofinanced by William Randolph Hearst and Arthur Brisbane. At year's end, on December 27, 1927, a new era in Broadway began at the Ziegfeld. Edna Ferber's *Show Boat* became the first musical production in which songs advanced the plot rather than delaying it. It was also the first time that white and black actors held the stage together in a serious show. In an era of "wonderful nonsense," the musical contained challenging themes about race and compelling storylines about personal convictions. *Show Boat* ran for 572 performances and became an American classic. It has been revived half a dozen times and adapted as a motion picture three times.

While *Show Boat* achieved immortality, the theater that bore the name of Florenz Ziegfeld Jr. didn't have a long life. It became a movie theater after the great showman's 1931 death. In 1944, Billy Rose purchased the playhouse and briefly resumed live theater there. In the Fifties, NBC rented it for television productions, such as the *Perry Como Show*. It was demolished in 1966, and an office tower built in its place. Not long after, a movie theater was built next door and given the Ziegfeld name.

## 12. Forty-ninth Street Theatre (demolished, 1940)

Designed by Herbert J. Krapp, the Forty-ninth Street Theatre opened during Christmas week, 1921. The only reason to remember this Shubert-owned theater is that on its stage every Round Table member participated in a one-night revue, in which they all wrote, sang, and acted in all the parts.

At the time, the hit show at the playhouse was *La Chauve-Souris*, a Russian-style revue that ran for more than five hundred performances. The Vicious Circle thought it would be fun to take over the theater on a Sunday night and invite their friends to an original production. They patterned it after the Russian show, and with a laugh, called it *No Siree*.

On April 30, 1922, the program kicked off with Broun as master of ceremonies, followed by the all-star male chorus: F.P.A., Benchley, Connelly, Kaufman, Toohey, and Woollcott. The group put on a parody of Eugene O'Neill, called *The Greasy Hag*, which they camped up with music by Arthur Samuels and Jascha Heifetz. A parody of *He Who Gets Slapped*, called *He Who Gets Flapped*—performed by

Under construction in 1921, the Forty-ninth Street Theatre was
demolished within twenty years. ◆ ◆ ◆

Sherwood and a chorus of dancing girls including some of the top
young actresses—brought the house down.

For that evening, Dorothy Parker wrote "The Everlastin' Ingénue
Blues," and another skit featured Harold Ross in a part that didn't
require him to take the stage, or even appear at all. When the curtain came down, one star emerged: Robert Benchley, who debuted
his "Treasurer's Report" there. The theater business audience had a
grand time and remembered it as one of the highlights of the season.

Another victim of the Great Depression, the theater became a
movie house in 1938, and in December 1940, fewer than twenty
years after it opened, it was demolished. A hotel stands there today.

# {6}

# MOVIES AND MICROPHONES

## Success on Screen and Air

*I don't understand the principle of the radio. Nor for that matter the telephone or the telegraph. Don't explain it to me; I don't get it.*

—FRANKLIN P. ADAMS

Books, newspapers. magazines, theater—nothing could contain the creative energy of the Algonquin Round Table. The group came into existence just as motion pictures were becoming a mainstream cultural force, and when radio broadcasting reached critical mass, the 44th Street talent pool found high-paying work. The Vicious Circle participated in every type of mass media in the first half of the twentieth century. Some even became television pioneers.

Franklin P. Adams on the hit radio show *Information Please.* ◆ ◆ ◆

Many first branched out from the printed word in motion pictures at studios in the Bronx, Brooklyn, Manhattan, and Queens. Screenwriters, including Herman Mankiewicz and Laurence Stallings, arrived in Hollywood before sound did, and became rich overnight. Connelly and Parker wrote titles for silent pictures. Benchley starred in *The Treasurer's Report*, a comedy short and probably the first all-talking film shown in theaters. Sherwood was one of the country's first critics of silent film. The technological advent of sound in the late Twenties provided more opportunities for writers and inspired them, as Parker wrote in "The Passionate Screen Writer to His Love" after moving to Hollywood:

> *Oh come, my love, and join with me*
> *The oldest infant industry.*
> *Come seek the bourne of palm and pearl,*
> *The lovely land of Boy-Meets-Girl,*
> *Come grace this lotus-laden shore,*
> *This Isle of Do-What's-Been-Done-Before.*
> *Come, curb the new, and watch the old win,*
> *Out where the streets are paved with Goldwyn.*

Radio also tapped the talents of the Vicious Circle. Among early radio stars was Franklin P. Adams, a weekly panelist on the hit quiz show, *Information Please*. George S. Kaufman and Deems Taylor also appeared on the program. Alexander Woollcott made a smooth transition in the Thirties from newspapers to radio, broadcasting from coast to coast on CBS. Many of the authors in the group found their material easily adapted to radio scripts: Benchley, Ferber, and Parker all cashed nice checks from radio producers for broadcasting dramatizations of their short stories.

But the gold standard of the entertainment business has always been gold: the Academy Award. Mankiewicz, Sherwood, and Stewart all won Oscars, and when the Round Table split up, almost a dozen members were Los Angeles residents. Here are radio and movie locations with ties to the Vicious Circle.

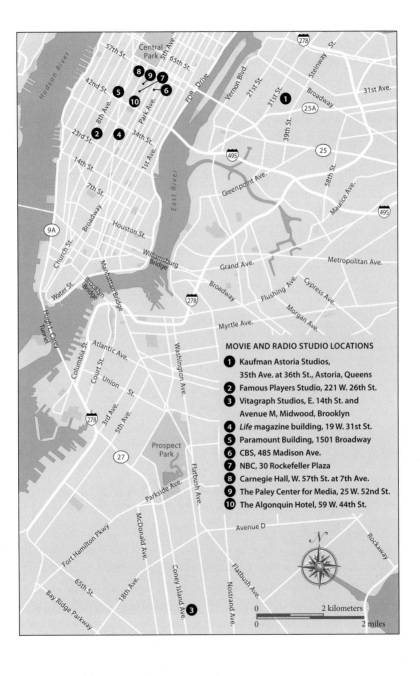

MOVIE AND RADIO STUDIO LOCATIONS

1. Kaufman Astoria Studios, 35th Ave. at 36th St., Astoria, Queens
2. Famous Players Studio, 221 W. 26th St.
3. Vitagraph Studios, E. 14th St. and Avenue M, Midwood, Brooklyn
4. *Life* magazine building, 19 W. 31st St.
5. Paramount Building, 1501 Broadway
6. CBS, 485 Madison Ave.
7. NBC, 30 Rockefeller Plaza
8. Carnegie Hall, W. 57th St. at 7th Ave.
9. The Paley Center for Media, 25 W. 52nd St.
10. The Algonquin Hotel, 59 W. 44th St.

## 1. PARAMOUNT–FAMOUS PLAYERS–LASKY STUDIO (KAUFMAN ASTORIA STUDIOS)

New York's most famous movie studio stands in Astoria, Queens, a twenty-five-minute subway ride from Times Square. Here Robert Benchley and the Marx Brothers made their classics. The original six-acre complex opened in 1919 as the Famous Players–Lasky Studio, with a stage just 220 feet wide. The company changed its name to Paramount Pictures soon after.

Having an East Coast studio meant that stars such as Clara Bow, W. C. Fields, Gloria Swanson, and Rudolph Valentino could make movies close to Manhattan without forcing stars to travel to Hollywood by train, which could take almost a week. From 1921 to 1927 more than a hundred silent films were made in Astoria.

The studio in 1920 and the backlot where Helen Kane filmed *Dangerous Dan McGrew* in 1929. ◆ ◆ ◆

The first Round Table member to make a "talkie" was Benchley. He shot *The Treasurer's Report* in late 1927 in Astoria. It was released in March 1928. Some film historians consider it the first all-talking picture, because *The Jazz Singer* was mostly silent. With the advent of sound, Broadway musicals were highly sought after. Paramount paid the Marx Brothers $100,000 in 1929 to make *The Cocoanuts*, which had been a big hit on Broadway and on the road. The brothers filmed their scenes in Astoria on days off from starring in *Animal Crackers*, which was playing at the Forty-fourth Street Theatre.

The script, by George S. Kaufman and Morrie Ryskind, closely followed the stage production. It debuted May 3, 1929, in Times Square at the Rialto Theatre and was a smash. The *Times* described Harpo as "content with a silence that has proved golden." As a follow-up the next year, the Marx brothers went back to Queens to film *Animal Crackers* with the same creative team. Set in an upscale Long Island residence, the comedy was also a hit at the Rialto when it opened on August 29, 1930. The studio stayed busy in the Thirties, but the Great Depression and cheaper production costs in Hollywood spelled the end of the studio's life.

Paramount sold it, and in 1942 the US Army Signal Corps took it over to make training films before abandoning the site after the war. New York City gained control in the Seventies, and the old studio was added to the National Register of Historic Places in 1978. In the Eighties, the site was developed as Kaufman Astoria Studios for TV and movie production. Since then, directors such as Woody Allen, Mike Nichols, and Oliver Stone have shot there. In 1988, the Museum of the Moving Image opened in one of the old studio buildings; it's the only museum in the country devoted solely to all aspects of filmmaking. In 2008 the museum started a $65 million expansion that doubled its size. Kaufman Astoria Studios isn't open to the public, but the museum is. Visit MovingImage.us for visitor information.

## 2. Famous Players Studio

In the silent-picture era, Chelsea was Manhattan's movie hub, and Hungarian-born furrier-turned-nickelodeon-chain operator Adolph Zukor was the city's first movie mogul. In 1912 he acquired the rights to show *Les Amours de la Reine Elizabeth* (*Queen Elizabeth*), a four-reel silent epic made in France starring fifty-seven-year-old Sarah Bernhardt. Its huge success prompted Zukor to found his own studio, which he called Famous Players in Famous Plays, at **221 West 26th Street,** in 1914. Among its roster of stars were three residents of the Algonquin: John Barrymore, Douglas Fairbanks, and Mary Pickford. Before Zukor moved his studio to Astoria in 1919, his films were shot in Chelsea. Among the Round Tablers to work for the moviemakers was Marc Connelly. Today the site is the location of Chelsea Studios, where Martha Stewart, Rachael Ray, and Tyra Banks produce their shows.

The studio in 1916. It was demolished in the Fifties to become large soundstages. ◆ ◆ ◆

### 3. VITAGRAPH STUDIOS

Margalo Gillmore was one of the few performers to run the acting gamut from silent movies to live television, and she did both in Brooklyn at Vitagraph Studios, located at **East 14th Street and Avenue M.** It was among the first movie studios built in the country, and one of the largest.

The American Vitagraph Company started in Lower Manhattan at **140 Nassau Street** at the dawn of moviemaking, in 1898. The company shot one-reel silent films on the roof, including the cleverly planned *The Burglar on the Roof.* In 1903 they moved offices to the Morse Building, **116 Nassau Street,** where a 1910 fire in their film vault nearly burned down the building. Around 1906, they launched operations in Midwood, Brooklyn, sparsely populated at the time (working farms still dotted the neighborhood).

Among the earliest Vitagraph stars before 1910 were John Bunny, the screen's first comedian, and Norma Talmadge, who lived nearby. The studio shot *Uncle Tom's Cabin* and *A Dixie Mother* that year. Not long after, the teenage Gillmore answered an ad looking for $5-a-day extras. She and her mother, actress Laura MacGillivray, took a series of streetcars and elevated trains to reach the country studio. They brought their own costumes and were shown the makeup department, which, as Gillmore later recalled, had unusual practices:

> We were herded into an ice-cold cement dressing room. The make-up man arrived and started to make us up. I had been looking forward to this, as my father had never allowed me to use lip rouge or powder, so I was somewhat surprised when white plaster was applied to my face and my lips were painted black. And there were black circles around my eyes ... all of us looking like candidates for Campbell's Funeral Parlor.

# 10 Films Tied to the Round Table

Edna Ferber and James Dean on the set of *Giant.* ◆ ◆ ◆

1. *The Big Parade* (1925), directed by the legendary King Vidor, was the first blockbuster war drama. Laurence Stalling based his screenplay on his combat experience in the US Marine Corps.

2. *A Star Is Born* (1934) landed Dorothy Parker one of her two Oscar nominations for the screenplay.

3. *How to Sleep* (1935) was an eleven-minute short starring Robert Benchley. It won the Oscar for best comedy short subject.

4. *A Night at the Opera* (1935), the Marx Brothers classic, was written by George S. Kaufman and Morrie Ryskind.

5. *The Philadelphia Story* (1940) earned Donald Ogden Stewart and Dalton Trumbo a screenplay Oscar while both were blacklisted.

6. *Citizen Kane* (1941) gave Herman J. Mankiewicz and Orson Welles an Oscar for best original screenplay. Mankiewicz drew on his time at the *New York World* for the story.

7. *The Best Years of Our Lives* (1946) won seven Academy Awards, including best writing, screenplay, for Robert E. Sherwood.

8. *It's A Wonderful Life* (1946) featured Dorothy Parker as an uncredited script doctor.

9. *Giant* (1956) starred James Dean, Rock Hudson, and Elizabeth Taylor in an adaptation of Edna Ferber's eponymous novel.

10. *High Society* (1956) showcased Margalo Gillmore playing alongside Grace Kelly, Frank Sinatra, and Bing Crosby in the classic musical.

The old studio smokestack is still a local landmark. ◆ ◆ ◆

Almost half a century later, Gillmore made the trip back to Brooklyn to appear on live television as Mrs. Darling in *Peter Pan*, starring Mary Martin.

Warner Bros. bought Vitagraph in 1925 and made films there until the Fifties, when NBC built a studio across the street in 1954, shooting *Another World* and *The Cosby Show* there. Vitagraph erected a large smokestack on the corner of Locust Avenue and East 115th Street with V-I-T-A-G-R-A-P-H emblazoned down the side, a landmark still visible today. The original Vitagraph building was sold and became the country's first Orthodox Jewish elementary school for girls.

## 4. *LIFE* MAGAZINE BUILDING

There is *Life*, and there is *LIFE*. The magazines share a name but are diametrically different. The original *Life* was a humorous weekly, published from 1883 to 1936. Its publisher was illustrator Charles Dana Gibson, creator of the classic Gibson Girl in the 1890s. John Held Jr. created sublime art for its covers. During the Jazz Age, *Life* was the bible for flappers and bootleggers alike.

Practically every Round Table member wrote for the magazine. Robert E. Sherwood became editor after he quit *Vanity Fair* in 1920.

Soon after, he turned his attention to reviewing silent pictures. Early on Sherwood recognized motion pictures as a new art form, delivering stinging or hilarious reviews. In 1926 he said of *Mantrap*: "An amusing tale of a triangle in the outdoors," and of *Nell Gwynne*: "Dorothy Gish manages to show off her

Once a magazine office, now a hotel. ◆ ◆ ◆

legs through the voluminous costumes of the Restoration period."

During the Depression, *Life* fell on hard times and folded when *Time* publisher Henry Luce paid $92,000 for the rights to the name in 1936. The building into which the magazine moved in 1894 is a Beaux-Arts gem designed by Carrère & Hastings. Over the door floats a limestone cherub and the word "Life," flanked by "Wit" and "Humor." Look up at the facade, and you'll see double "L" monograms and a limestone panel that spells "Life" on the sixth-floor balcony. Today it is the Herald Square Hotel. (A 1995 renovation destroyed the roof and chimneys.)

## 5. PARAMOUNT THEATRE BUILDING

Dorothy Parker and Robert Benchley both worked for Paramount Pictures, headquartered in New York. The Marx Brothers made deals with studio boss Adolph Zukor here, too. Chicago architects Rapp & Rapp—brothers who created more than a hundred movie palaces across the country during Hollywood's Golden Age—designed the

Opened in 1927, the tower once had a public observation deck from which to view Times Square. ◆ ◆ ◆

twenty-nine-story Paramount Building. Five-pointed stars, just as in the Paramount Pictures logo, mark the hours on its giant four-faced clock, and the illuminated glass globe is visible from New Jersey. At one time the Paramount Theatre was located inside; it has since been demolished. The building opened in 1926. In the early days of CBS radio, the network was so small that it rented a floor in the building in 1927. Today the Hard Rock Cafe occupies the ground floor.

At **315 West 99th Street** stands the Paramount apartment building, built in 1900. Zukor lived here and took the name for his studio from it.

## 6. CBS

Alexander Woollcott loved to pontificate. He was a ham, a showman, and a natural as a radio broadcaster. He also notoriously recycled magazine articles and sold them to two and even three publications. Getting a radio show allowed him to retell those same stories to another audience, and saved his career. From 1930 to 1943, Woollcott worked on the top floor in Studio One of the CBS Building. In 1930, the twenty-four-story Columbia Broadcasting Building was completed for the two-year-old CBS radio network at **485 Madison Avenue** to designs by J. E. R. Carpenter. This was CBS's home until 1965, when the company moved to the thirty-eight-story CBS Building designed by Eero Saarinen on Sixth Avenue and 52nd Street, nicknamed "Black Rock."

## 7. NBC

Franklin P. Adams was a veteran newspaper columnist with thirty-five years' experience when the *Herald Tribune* decided not to renew his contract in 1937. With an encyclopedic knowledge of literature

# Round Tablers in the Library of Congress National Film Registry

Motion pictures to which members of the Round Table contributed and that the Library of Congress has added to the National Film Registry to be preserved in the national archives for perpetuity:

- *A Night at the Opera* (Harpo Marx, costar; George S. Kaufman, screenplay)

- *Citizen Kane* (Herman Mankiewicz, writer)

- *Duck Soup* (Harpo Marx, costar)

- *Giant* (Edna Ferber, writer)

- *Show Boat* (Edna Ferber, writer)

- *It's A Wonderful Life* (Dorothy Parker, uncredited script doctor)

- *The Big Parade* (Laurence Stallings, writer)

- *The Philadelphia Story* (Donald Ogden Stewart, adapted screenplay)

- *The Sex Life of the Polyp* (Robert Benchley, writer and star)

- *The Sound of Music* (Peggy Wood, costar)

Mayor Fiorello La Guardia and F. P. A. on *Information Please.* ◆ ◆ ◆

and trivia and a family of five to support during the height of the Great Depression, the offer to be a regular panelist on a radio quiz show came as a blessing. Radio saved him, and *Information Please* was the last hurrah of his brilliant career.

The format was simple but brilliant: Listeners mailed in questions. If the question stumped a panel of experts, the listener won a small cash prize. The show was unrehearsed and conducted before a live studio audience. The thirty-minute program moved like lightning, and experts and guests had to answer quickly. On May 17, 1938, *Information Please* debuted on the NBC Blue Network (later ABC). Clifton Fadiman, a literary critic who wrote for *The New Yorker*, was master of ceremonies. The show became an overnight success, and more than 25,000 questions poured into the studios weekly.

The International Building of
Rockefeller Center is excavated
in 1934. ◆ ◆ ◆

One question put to F.P.A. in 1938 was to finish the Joe Miller gag, "Who was that lady I saw you with last night?" To which he replied, "There are two answers: That was no lady, that was my wife. And the other is that was no lady that was your wife." The show continued for ten years, mostly on NBC. Over time, just about every Round Table member appeared as a guest.

NBC has always been associated with Rockefeller Center. The area bounded by Fifth and Sixth Avenues from 48th to 51st Streets contained numerous speakeasies before their demolition in 1930. John D. Rockefeller Jr., son of the founder of Standard Oil, owned the land and helped to create the landmark. NBC has called 30 Rockefeller Plaza home since the building was completed in 1933, spanning corporate ownership from General Electric to Comcast. More than a dozen buildings form the complex today, with "30 Rock" as the centerpiece. Radio studios were the original tenants (hence, Radio City), and now, television studios. The Art Deco buildings are landmarks both inside and out.

## 8. CARNEGIE HALL

Designed by William B. Tuthill, Carnegie Hall—one of the nation's finest concert halls—has a Roman brick and terra-cotta exterior designed in an Italian Renaissance style.

Steel magnate Andrew Carnegie financed the project, and it opened in 1891 with a concert conducted by Tchaikovsky in his American debut.

When radio networks became national broadcasters in the late Twenties, some of the live programming was classical music. Symphonies and orchestras dominated as networks tried to reach upper-class listeners. William S. Paley signed the New York Philharmonic to CBS in a major coup and gave the network enormous prestige.

Beginning in 1936, Deems Taylor served as commentator during intermissions. Already a star composer and conductor, Taylor had been a newspaper music critic but never a broadcaster. He was enormously successful at CBS, and soon found himself giving weekly music lectures to a huge audience during Sunday-afternoon concerts in Carnegie Hall. He helped listeners to understand what they were hearing, and encouraged a generation to appreciate classical music. Taylor also introduced listener questions, interviewed orchestra members during intermission, and brought the whole experience of classical music into the nation's living rooms. A broadcaster for more than ten years, Taylor became the country's best-known authority on music.

The building was saved from a wrecking ball in 1960, and in recent years has undergone multimillion-dollar renovations. Today the Isaac Stern Auditorium, the main performance hall, seats 2,800.

## 9. The Museum of Broadcasting (The Paley Center for Media)

The media archives here have many Round Table connections. Visitors can listen to F.P.A. on *Information Please* (NBC), with guests such as Harpo Marx (who whistled his answers), Dorothy Parker, Frank Sullivan, and Deems Taylor; Alexander Woollcott's broadcasts as the *Town Crier* (CBS); and early television shows, such as *Mama* with Peggy Wood (CBS), *Peter Pan* with Margalo Gillmore (NBC), and *This Is Show Business* (CBS) with panelist George S. Kaufman.

CBS Chairman William S. Paley founded the Museum of Broadcasting in 1975. In 1991 the museum opened a new building at **25 West 52nd Street,** designed by Philip Johnson. In 2007 the Museum of Television & Radio changed its name to the Paley Center for Media. The center is open to the public and contains nearly 150,000 programs and ads dating back to 1918. Learn more at PaleyCenter.org.

# THE RISE OF *THE NEW YORKER*

## From Hell's Kitchen to Midtown

*That piece is worth coming back to work for. It will turn out to be a memorable one, or I am a fish.*
—HAROLD ROSS

*The New Yorker* and the Algonquin Round Table go together like gin and tonic. Without the Vicious Circle, the magazine wouldn't exist today. Its early success came because founding editor Harold Ross, a virtual unknown when he landed in New York in 1919, had personal relationships with the Round Table members. Described as a "genius in disguise," Ross was a master manipulator and wildly successful at turning personal relationships into material for his magazine.

At age twenty-five, Ross joined the army in San Francisco, and he might have returned there after the war. But after befriending New Yorkers in Paris, such as Franklin P. Adams and Alexander Woollcott, the idea of continuing his career in Manhattan appealed to him. The real draw, though, was Jane Grant, with whom Ross had fallen deeply in love in Paris. He followed her back to New York, and they married two years after the war. When he returned to civilian life, Ross abandoned newspapers and took up magazine editing, which paid the bills while he planned bigger things. Grant pushed, energized, and encouraged Ross to pursue their dream of publishing a magazine. As she said after his death, "Ross had not yet been bitten by ambition."

In 1925 Jane Grant and Harold Ross sat for celebrity photographer Nickolas Muray. ◆ ◆ ◆

*The New Yorker* was dreamed up in Hell's Kitchen and launched in office space within spitting distance of the Algonquin Hotel. For nine decades its impact on the city and the nation has been profound. These are the locations of *The New Yorker*.

## 1. Home of Harold Ross, Jane Grant, Alexander Woollcott

No place is more important to the launch of *The New Yorker* than **412 West 47th Street,** where Jane Grant and Harold Ross cooked up the magazine in their second-floor bedroom in 1924. The couple married in early 1920 but didn't immediately move in together. Strapped for funds, Heywood Broun and Ruth Hale took the newlyweds in for a summer, and the odd couple briefly took a suite at the Algonquin. Their first apartment was a walk-up they rented for two years at **231 West 58th Street,** near Central Park. It lay above an auto parts shop, which probably explains why Grant pushed Ross to buy something elsewhere. Grant wanted an apartment; Ross a house. They compromised, settling on a duplex in Hell's Kitchen.

At the time, the neighborhood was still a little rough, and the house stood just west of the Ninth Avenue El. Grant didn't want to move there: "Hell's Kitchen was, in fact, an Irish-bordered-by-Negro slum," she said. But the price was right: $5,000 down, and an $11,000 mortgage. She got over her prejudices. The couple undertook a massive renovation of the twin houses and drew up plans to start a cooperative, with the intention to sell shares to friends. The first taker was Alexander Woollcott; three other acquaintances became renters.

At the housewarming party in 1922, the neighbors on West 47th Street got a taste of what to expect from the new tenants. Grant

Woollcott tried to make the house his fiefdom, to no avail. ◆ ◆ ◆

lined up a private bootlegger to supply the spirits. Just about every member of the Round Table along with two hundred guests attended. Charles MacArthur and Dorothy Parker helped to fund a street carrousel for the neighborhood kids, and in the living room Grant set up a roulette wheel and a table for *chemin de fer.*

In the coming months and years, "412" became a special house for the group. The twenty-five-foot-square community room hosted marathon poker parties and long discussions that would eventually launch *The New Yorker.* A communal kitchen often fed close to fifty on weekends, requiring Grant, Ross, and Woollcott to employ a staff of cooks and servants. Iron steps led to the back garden, where the group installed a fountain and patio. Chinese lanterns lit the backyard for parties.

In 1924 Ross quit the American Legion magazine he was editing. While living in the Hell's Kitchen house, he lined up the resources to launch what became *The New Yorker.* While Grant worked as a reporter on the *Times* and sold pieces to the *Saturday Evening Post,* the couple salted his salary away to finance their new venture. In its early days, Ross met with editors at all hours in the house, even while he was shaving. E. B. White talked to Ross over dinner at "412," and editorial plans were drawn up there.

# Highlights

Some of the most memorable moments that occurred at 412 West 47th Street in the Twenties included:

- At one soirée, Woollcott asked Peggy Wood to lean out a second-floor window and entertain party guests below with a scene from *Romeo and Juliet*.

- Scott and Zelda Fitzgerald, at the zenith of their fame, attended parties here.

- George Gershwin previewed "Rhapsody in Blue," then a work in progress, on the secondhand piano.

- Edna St. Vincent Millay read her new poems for the group.

- Ring and Ellis Lardner were among the most popular of all visitors.

- Beatrice Lillie and Ethel Barrymore, the most popular actresses of the day, performed for partygoers.

- Irving Berlin liked trying out his new songs for the appreciative audience.

Stacked in the apartment were manuscripts to read, cartoons to review, and dummies for upcoming issues. The house intertwined with the life of *The New Yorker*, as well as Grant and Ross. Just two years after the magazine launched in 1925, the marriage collapsed. On August 6, 1928, they permanently separated. The couple went their separate ways, and the house was sold.

In the Sixties, Grant believed "412" was haunted: "The ghost—a male figure—is said to appear mostly on the second floor back, Aleck's old room, and later Ross's bedroom. I hope he has as much fun there now as we did during those five years."

## 2. First Office, 1925–1935

The sixteen-story building opened around 1910 and has 145,000 square feet of office space. Starrett & Van Vleck designed it. Goldwin Starrett, a founder of the firm, had designed the Algonquin Hotel. The developers were James T. Lee, grandfather of Jacqueline Kennedy, and his partner, Charles R. Fleischmann.

In 1924 Jane Grant and Harold Ross started to build the company that would create *The New Yorker*. Grant and Ross showed their mock-up of the first issue to potential advertisers, investors, writers, and subscribers. Ross fibbed that he had lined up "advisory editors" such as Connelly, Kaufman, Parker, and Woollcott. They landed their biggest investor, Raoul H. Fleischmann, whom Grant had met while playing bridge. Raoul Fleischmann was the scion of a wealthy family that controlled the General Baking Company, one of the country's largest bread manufacturers. A benefit of Fleischmann's cash was that he had access to free office space one block from the Algonquin. One of his older brothers was an owner of **25 West 45th Street, the Century Building.**

Both Edna Ferber and F.P.A. contributed stories to *The New Yorker* in its debut year. ◆ ◆ ◆

The magazine debuted on Thursday, February 19, 1925, and was dated the following Saturday. The cover price was 15 cents, and the first printing was 15,000 copies. By late spring, circulation had dropped to 8,000, then dipped to a low of 2,700. The future looked rocky. James Thurber called it "the outstanding flop of 1925." Ross and Grant burned through all their money, so Fleischmann had to pour more in. He nearly pulled the plug and let the magazine fold. However, at the May 1925 wedding of F.P.A. and Esther Sayles Root, Fleischmann told Ross that they would continue. The magazine would turn a profit three years later.

For the ten years that the magazine was edited in this building, scores of legends walked its halls. E. B. White joined in 1926, and James Thurber a year later. In 1928 John O'Hara started a forty-year association with the magazine. Adams kicked in for issue number 1 with a satirical piece on writing fiction, contributing to the magazine until 1949. Benchley, one of the highest-paid humorists in the country, wrote drama reviews and press criticism. When he went to Hollywood, Parker filled in for him. Connelly passed along humorous sketches and "Talk of the Town" contributions from 1926 to 1954. Kaufman wrote thirteen pieces, between 1935 and 1960.

Ferber gave Ross a two-page profile of journalist William Allen White in issue 15 in May 1925, when only a few thousand people were reading it. Heywood Broun's first article for the magazine was a hilarious 1927 profile of himself, written in the third person. Margaret Leech helped make "Profiles" a unique new form of journalism, and wrote early ones in 1927–28 about female newsmakers such as Anne Morgan, who organized World War I relief efforts. Herman Mankiewicz attended the birth of the magazine and wrote drama reviews and marketing sales copy.

Parker anonymously wrote the debut issue's theater page. ("Say what you will—and who has a better right?—about the present theatrical season, it has been a great little year for sex.") Parker was a mainstay of the magazine until 1963, writing poems, short stories, drama reviews, book reviews, and casuals. In 1927 she was handed the reins of the "Recent Books" column, and assumed the alias "Constant Reader." Parker's most famous review was of *The House at Pooh Corner* by A. A. Milne. The Englishman got under her skin, and spying "hummy" on the page pushed her over the edge: "It is that word 'hummy,' my darlings, that marks the first place in *The House at Pooh Corner* at which Tonstant Weader fwowed up."

Murdock Pemberton gave Ross a poem for the third issue. He wrote for the magazine until 1961. Without any formal fine art education, he was *The New Yorker*'s first art critic. Sherwood, editor of *Life*, profiled director Cecil B. DeMille in 1925. The next year he wrote about silent-movie star Harold Lloyd. Frank Sullivan had the longest association of any member of the Vicious Circle. He wrote humor pieces from March 1925 until December 1974.

Deems Taylor wrote a 1929 profile of conductor Walter Damrosch, and Peggy Wood, an actress turned writer, contributed to "Talk of the Town." Woollcott wrote almost 250 pieces for the magazine, from 1925 to 1939. He created the "Shouts & Murmurs" department in 1929 and wrote it almost weekly for five years. Woollcott was legendary among the staff when it came to how difficult it was to edit and fact-check his copy. He and Ross had an acrimonious split, and Woollcott quit.

Other greats who came to the first location of the magazine in this era were Ogden Nash and S. J. Perelman in 1930, illustrator Charles Addams in 1933, and critic Edmund Wilson in 1934. In 1935 the staff outgrew the space and moved one block away. Since *The New Yorker* moved out, the building has housed many interesting tenants over the decades, including William F. Buckley's Conservative Party, and the Samuel French Company.

### 3. SECOND OFFICE, 1935–1991

At the nadir of the Great Depression, *The New Yorker* was doing so well that it outgrew its office space. The magazine moved from West 45th to West 44th Street in 1935. The official name of the location is the **National Association Building.** The twenty-story tower was designed by Starrett & Van Vleck, and opened in 1920. The magazine eventually occupied seven floors in the building, with editors on floors eighteen through twenty.

For almost sixty years *The New Yorker* was edited from this building that confusingly opens onto both 43rd and 44th Streets. From the elevators of **25 West 43rd Street,** it takes five minutes to reach

# The Pomona-Pulitzer Crusade

*The New Yorker* has a long history of sticking its nose into matters of frivolity around New York City, and the magazine loves a good crusade. E. B. White complained vociferously about advertising in Grand Central Terminal, and editor Harold Ross, a commuter, testified at a city hearing against public address announcements in the terminal.

The magazine also took up the cause of the dirty bronze statue of Pomona, goddess of abundance, located outside the Plaza Hotel in Grand Army Plaza at the southeastern corner of Central Park. When *New York World* publisher Joseph Pulitzer died in 1912,

Pomona in all her glory; Scott & Zelda Fitzgerald jumped into the fountain after their wedding. ◆ ◆ ◆

he bequeathed $50,000 to build it. Carrère & Hastings designed the Italian Renaissance–style fountain, which was dedicated in 1916. But in *The New Yorker* of April 18, 1931, poet Arthur Guiterman complained that the fountain was a mess. The last stanza of "Letter to Mr. Pulitzer" reads:

> *One hates to speak this way about a lady,*
> *But she is obviously much too shady;*
> *Though still quite young, a good bit under thirty,*
> *No nymph was ever quite so black and dirty*
> *In all New York; so you, sir, as her guardian*
> *(You see I'm Mid-Victorian, not Edwardian),*
> *Should personally scrub her form and face in*
> *The sudsy foam of her own fountain basin.*

A few weeks later the magazine published a response by Pulitzer's son, Ralph, publisher of the *World*:

> *For know! The lady's guardians ad litem,*
> *Aroused by her attempts to mock and spite 'em,*
> *Have joined the city in a contribution*
> *To give her an immaculate ablution;*
> *To scrub her from her head, with all its wet locks,*
> *Clear down her contours to her very fetlocks.*

Pulitzer donated $30,000 to restore the statue. Doris Doscher, the model who posed for sculptor Karl Bitter as Pomona, wrote to the *New York Times*: "I want to take this opportunity to offer my thanks to Mr. Pulitzer for enabling me to again stand exalted—and scrubbed—above the grounds on Fifth Avenue, generously spurting precious, clear water—flush, in these times of dried-up prosperity."

The saga of the statue and Pulitzer Fountain is a long-running city drama. It was renovated in 1971, but, due to faulty plumbing, went dry for six years in the Eighties. In 1989, $3.3 million was raised privately to restore it yet again.

the lobby of the Algonquin Hotel. In this era, the magazine rose to international prominence. Ross was editor until his death in 1951, when his trusted lieutenant, William Shawn, took command for the next thirty-five years.

During these glory years the magazine cemented its reputation, and those elevators played a part in the magazine's legend. Ross forbade staff from talking to him on the ride up or down the twenty floors, his theory being that he didn't want to tip off other passengers that they were riding with the editor of *The New Yorker*. The magazine's lease quirkily required that a manually operated elevator and operator had to be on duty.

Contributors drew scores of cartoons on the walls of the art department. James Thurber also drew cartoons on office walls, but one of the most memorable was in a hallway: a man breezily walking along, while around a corner a woman waited with a club in hand to whack him.

In 1991, six years after being sold to Advance Publications, the staff vacated the offices and moved sixty feet south, to **20 West 43rd Street.** They lasted there for about ten years. In 2000, the magazine moved to the twentieth and twenty-first floors of **4 Times Square,** on the corner of 42nd Street and Seventh Avenue. This forty-eight-story building (nickname: The Death Star) is also home to *GQ*, *Vanity Fair*, and *Vogue*. In 2015 *The New Yorker* is scheduled to relocate downtown to **One World Trade Center, at 285 Fulton Street,** with the rest of Condé Nast.

## 4. Alexander Woollcott Apartment, Wit's End

Alexander Woollcott wrecked a fantastic living situation with friends Jane Grant and Harold Ross, who should have received medals for putting up with the most difficult roommate of all time. Woollcott

The Campanile, 450 East 52nd Street. The breakfasts that Aleck Woollcott held here were legendary. ◆ ◆ ◆

complained about everything at 412 West 47th Street, from the food to the party guests. Matters came to a head in the summer of 1927, not long before Grant and Ross separated. Grant asked Woollcott to leave because Ross despised personal conflicts.

The rotund critic decamped twenty blocks uptown, taking the tableware and household help with him. He moved into the **Hotel des Artistes, 1 West 67th Street,** a 1918 landmark that faces Central Park. He lived there for about three years; during this time his newspaper days ended, and his radio broadcasting career began. With his fat paychecks from CBS, Woollcott set up shop in the **Campanile, 450 East 52nd Street,** one of the most famous apartment buildings on the East River.

Franklin P. Adams suggested that Woollcott name his place "Ocowoica," a made-up Native American word meaning The-Little-Apartment-on-the-East-River-That-It-Is-Difficult-to-Find-a-Taxi-Cab-Near. But Dorothy Parker came up with the name that stuck: Wit's End. Woollcott's third-floor apartment had a commanding view of the East River and overlooked a small garden below (lost when FDR Drive was constructed in 1938).

Wit's End became Woollcott's most famous address. Sunday breakfasts were the highlight, with Woollcott hosting in his pajamas and bathrobe, brunch filling up most of the day. He served his favorite dishes: eggs, sausage, French toast with maple syrup, pancakes, and jelly donuts. Anything that would clog your arteries, Woollcott served. Among the visitors here were Charlie Chaplin and Thornton Wilder. Although he lived alone—one of the rare occasions in his life—his friends weren't far away. Peggy Leech and Ralph Pulitzer also lived in the building, and Alice Duer Miller lived across the hall. When his parties overflowed his space, he would walk over, open her door (unannounced), and the guests would spill over into her apartment. Frank Sullivan lived around the corner, and Parker took an apartment next door to Wit's End at **444 East 52nd Street.**

Designed by Van Wart & Wein, the Campanile opened in 1930. When it opened, the building sat on the river's edge, and the Montauk Yacht Club moored its boats to the Campanile's private dock. The exclusive fourteen-story co-op has fewer than twenty apartments and sits at the end of the block. Woollcott lived at the Campanile through the Thirties. But as his fame and wealth increased, he moved to **10 Gracie Square** on the Upper East Side.

## 5. GRAND CENTRAL TERMINAL

*The New Yorker* has devoted more attention to Grand Central Terminal than any other place in New York City. Since 1925, more than five hundred items and cartoons have made mention of the landmark destination. Since the magazine's inception, the train station has been a ten-minute walk away and a constant source of inspiration for writers and cartoonists. Key staff members and contributors were commuters: F.P.A., Benchley, Ross, Thurber, and White, among them. Passing through the place ten times a week, they were bound to collect material.

In the magazine's first year, Grand Central starred in "Talk of the Town" pieces and a cartoon by Joseph Fannell of flappers and men in boaters in the main concourse:

Watch-watching, harried, breathless, snatchy talkers.
They pass—commute, inglorious New Yorkers.

Cartoonists adore the four-faced clock above the information booth. A 1934 Helen E. Hokinson drawing shows a well-dressed woman pointing angrily to it, asking a porter, "Is that clock right?" The next year Charles Addams drew the same booth, without a caption, with a fortune-teller inside it.

In 1932, Thurber went inside the Grand Central office of John W. Campbell, who had a luxurious space tucked into a hidden corner of the station. "It's sixty feet long, thirty feet wide; the ceiling is twenty-five feet above you. At a huge carved desk at the far end of the room sits Mr. Campbell, looking tiny." Today, that space is the Campbell Apartment, a cocktail lounge and bar.

Grand Central Terminal sees almost 100 million visitors annually. ◆ ◆ ◆

The writer with the earliest affection for the station was E. B. White. Grand Central served as a constant source of inspiration for him. He wrote about train schedules, overheard conversations, station signs, and little annoyances. (He once called the New York, New Haven & Hartford Railroad "unimaginative" for failing to post the 5:10 to Stamford clearly.)

In 1949, White landed Ross in every newspaper in town. The dispute was broadcast ads and public address announcements in the station, which left White aghast and bemoaning "the racket in the Terminal." Ross, who commuted between New York and Connecticut, must have agreed. He was asked to testify before the New York State Public Service Commission because the magazine had begun a letter-writing campaign against the station's music and announcements. Ultimately he won, and that silence continues today.

# {8}

# SPEAKEASIES AND BROTHELS

## The Heady Twenties

*Donald Ogden Stewart called Robert Benchley a typical man about town because "At 1 a.m. you can find Bob sitting at '21,' at 5 p.m. you can find Bob sitting at '21,' and at midnight you can find Bob sitting at '21.'"*

It's impossible to separate the Algonquin Round Table from speakeasy lore. The heyday of the Vicious Circle began and ended during Prohibition, the grand experiment that failed so mightily. From the day it began in 1920 to its end in 1933, obedience of the law by New Yorkers was a farce. From 1921 to 1923, 7,000 arrests for alcohol-related offenses resulted in only 17 convictions. The number of city "speaks" was hard to pin down even then; estimates ranged from an incredible 32,000 to a whopping 100,000.

A respectable speakeasy had a limited selection for drinkers: draught beer, ale, and anything that could be mixed with gin, rye, whiskey, or bourbon. Rare was the place that served cocktails with more than three ingredients, which proved too much trouble to the bartender. Most popular were the Bronx, Gin Fizz, Whiskey Highball, and a Jack Rose. Prices varied—"[n]ormal being $1 a drink, $1.25 for a *good* drink," Lois Long wrote in *The New Yorker*.

Manhattan speakeasies of the Twenties had colorful names: the Furnace, the Hyena, the Ha! Ha!, the Jail Club, the Peek Inn.

Texas Guinan, queen of the nightclubs, didn't live to see the repeal of Prohibition. ◆ ◆ ◆

Harlem had the low-down Drool Inn and the Hot Feet. Duke Ellington drew white audiences to the Cotton Club. The Casanova had Morton Downey and Helen Kane, the singer who inspired Betty Boop. The Club Pansy featured drag queens. In September 1923, agents raided **Peter's Blue Hour at 157 West 49th Street.** Customers threw chairs, hard bread rolls, and wet spaghetti at the men. The notorious joint was padlocked for a year in 1928.

In 1929 at the **Swanee Club at 253 West 125th Street** in Harlem, Evelyn Nesbit Thaw was arrested and hauled in. She was "The Girl on the Velvet Swing" over whom Harry K. Thaw infamously killed Stanford White on the roof of the old Madison Square Garden. She was charged with possession and sale of liquor. As Stanley Walker wrote, "At prohibition, whatever glamour Miss Nesbit had once was gone."

Of those in the group who wrote about alcohol in their work, Parker was an expert; she wrote from experience. She sold "Just a Little One" to Harold Ross, which he published in the May 12, 1928, issue of *The New Yorker*:

This is a nice highball, isn't it? Well, well, well to think of me having real Scotch; I'm out of the bush leagues at last. Are you going to have another one? Well, I shouldn't like to see you

Racy entertainment at a speak of the era. ◆ ◆ ◆

drinking all by yourself, Fred. Solitary drinking is what causes half the crime in the country. That's what's responsible for the failure of prohibition. But, please, Fred, tell him to make mine just a little one. Make it awfully weak; just cambric Scotch.

These are the speakeasies and other debauched locations associated with the Vicious Circle.

## 1. Tony's

In a February 1929 cartoon titled "Organizational Chart of *The New Yorker*" drawn by Julian de Miskey, Morton the Office Boy lies at the center of a flow chart. The publisher is connected directly only to the water cooler and Europe, and not far away lies a box labeled

**SPEAKEASY LOCATIONS**

1. Tony's, 65 W. 49th St.
2. Jack and Charlie's Puncheon Grotto, 42 W. 49th St.
3. The "21" Club, 21 W. 52nd St.
4. Club Intime, 205 W. 54th St.
5. The El Fey Club, 123 W. 45th St.
6. The Silver Slipper Club, 201 W. 48th St.
7. Midtown Speakeasies, 50th St. and 7th Ave.
8. Polly Adler's Brothel, 57 W. 58th St.
9. The Algonquin Hotel, 59 W. 44th St.

Central Park

W. 59th St.
W. 58th St.
W. 57th St.
W. 56th St.
W. 55th St.
W. 54th St
W. 53rd St.
W. 52nd St.
W. 51st St.
W. 50th St.
W. 49th St.
W. 48th St.
W. 47th St.
W. 46th St.
W. 45th St.
W. 44th St.
W. 43rd St.
W. 42nd St.
W. 41st St.
W. 40th St.
W. 39th St.
W. 38th St.
W. 37th St.

8th Ave.
Broadway
7th Ave.
6th Ave.
5th Ave.

E. 55th St.
E. 54th St.
E. 53rd St.
E. 52nd St.
E. 51st St.
E. 50th St.
E. 49th St.
E. 48th St.
E. 47th St.
E. 46th St.
E. 45th St.
E. 44th St.
E. 41st St.
E. 40th St.

Park Ave.
Vanderbilt Ave.
Madison Ave.

Bryant Park

Broadway
Avenue of the Americas

N

0       0.25 kilometer
0       0.25 mile

"Department for the Control of Artists." In the lower right corner of the schematic, a tiny doorway sits outside the office, marked "Tony's." This was **Tony Soma's speakeasy, 65 West 49th Street,** the preferred speak for the office staff.

Beloved by Marc Connelly, Dorothy Parker, and Harold Ross, Tony's was the ultimate speakeasy, where the regulars were writers, Broadway stars, and gangsters. Presiding over it was proprietor Tony Soma, an Italian immigrant who had started his career by waiting tables at the old Knickerbocker Hotel. At Tony's, Parker delivered one of her most immortal lines. A bartender asked her what she was having. "Not much fun," came her acid reply.

Tony Soma was the most genial of speakeasy owners. ◆ ◆ ◆

Benchley had his first social drink at Tony's. He was with Parker and Donald Ogden Stewart when he finally gave in, at age thirty-one, and joined the crowd. The poison he picked was an Orange Blossom (gin, orange juice, and a teaspoon of sugar). Benchley may have made a sour face, but he drank it down. His friends asked what he thought. "I think that this place ought to be closed down by the law," he replied. Later, Benchley and Stewart pulled a comic stunt outside Tony's during a rainstorm. They ducked underneath a passerby's umbrella, grabbed his arms, and told him, "Yale Club, please!"

Due to the redevelopment of Rockefeller Center, Soma had to move his bar in 1929. Today Christie's auction house occupies his prime spot.

# Tony Soma, Beloved Speakeasy Proprietor

Dapper speakeasy owner Tony Soma was beloved by his customers. ◆ ◆ ◆

Of the thousands of speakeasies in New York, Tony's stood out as the preferred destination for actors, editors, and writers. Tony Soma had such a sterling reputation five years after Prohibition ended, the *Knickerbocker News* recalled, "They call him THE Tony because of the confusion that existed in Prohibition days. At least 200 Antonios ran speakeasies, and whenever a date was arranged at Tony's, the invariable inquiry was, 'Which one?' The most authentic place, however, was THE Tony's, and to this day his name is prefixed by the capitalized article."

Soma emigrated from northern Italy and fell into the illegal booze business when he started selling wine to go with the dishes his sister was cooking for friends in his home in the early Twenties. With a charming personality and a product everyone wanted, he was soon in business.

In addition to the Vicious Circle, scores of other boldface names became avowed regulars, including Humphrey Bogart, Gary Cooper, Gypsy Rose Lee, John O'Hara, and Arnold Rothstein. Soma was so well known in New York that in 1934, the *Sun* asked him what his favorite Broadway shows were. First was *As You Desire Me*, then *Mary of Scotland*, and third was *American Dream*.

He moved his speakeasy from 49th to 52nd and reopened in 1934, adding a restaurant, Tony's Wife, next door. Business was so good that later he consolidated and ran a jazz café and cabaret. Among the jazz and blues stars Soma booked were Victoria Spivey and Mabel Mercer, who sang there during World War II.

During Prohibition, he fought against federal agents—who raided his establishment but never landed a conviction—and Rockefeller Center. Two of his locations fell to the wrecking ball for redevelopment. Soma moved a final time, and from 1947 to 1976 he operated **Tony's and Tony's Wife at 150 East 55th Street,** where the three-martini lunch began. He suffered personal setbacks as well. In 1927, his eight-year-old son, George, died of pneumonia. In 1932 his wife, Angelica Fantoni, died of rheumatic fever. Their son, Philip, was three months old, and daughter, Enrica "Ricki" Soma, was four years old.

As a teenager, Ricki danced as a ballerina in George Balanchine's company. Later she was the fourth wife of director John Huston, with whom she had two children: Angelica and Tony, who both became major Hollywood stars. Years later, granddaughter Angelica Huston recalled one of his aphorisms: "Through the knowledge of me, I wish to share my happiness with you!"

In 1934 Tony Soma married Dorothy Fraser and had three more children: Linda, Anthony Jr., and Fraser. He retired to Miller Place, Long Island, and died in 1979 at the age of eighty-nine, following a house fire.

## 2. Jack and Charlie's Puncheon Grotto

In 1926, the Algonquin crowd started frequenting a new speakeasy run by cousins Jack Kriendler and Charlie Berns. The partners had done well in the Village, running a speakeasy so popular that Mayor Jimmy Walker was a visitor. They moved their business to the row of brownstones at **42 West 49th Street** and dubbed it the **Puncheon Grotto.** Like many speakeasies, it was also known by the owners' names. Lasting four years, it had a big iron gate, a peephole, and the best booze on the black market—"the good stuff," smuggled from Canada. The speakeasy also had a chef and dishes that set new standards in the trade: fresh crab, brook trout, bouillabaisse stew, and filet mignon served on red-and-white-checked tablecloths.

Robert Benchley and Charles MacArthur on the town. ◆ ◆ ◆

Jack and Charlie's became one of the most popular speaks in town, and most of the Round Table became diehard regulars. They could bump into F. Scott Fitzgerald, H. L. Mencken, Will Rogers, actors, ballplayers, and politicos. Only those known to the house, those personally introduced by a regular, or the type that Jack and Charlie wanted to attract were allowed in the Puncheon. Chorus girls were admitted to draw in more customers.

After Black Tuesday and the Wall Street Crash of 1929, patrons lost millions, but the club hardly felt it. The end for Jack and Charlie's came not in a Prohibition raid but from a wrecking ball: The Puncheon stood in the middle of what became Rockefeller Center. The curtain fell on December 31, 1929, during a raucous party. Guests were given hammers and allowed to destroy the place. A policeman even rode his horse through the party as the club was demolished. Jack and Charlie's Puncheon Grotto reopened as "21" on West 52nd Street in 1930. The speakeasy once stood roughly where NBC's *Today* show studio is located today.

## 3. The "21" Club

The day after the Puncheon Grotto was destroyed, Jack and Charlie hauled its massive iron gate three blocks uptown. It's still there. Kriendler and Berns bought a single-family townhouse at **21 West 52nd Street** and set up the bar and about ten tables on the first floor. Later they expanded to the rest of the house and the two adjoining houses. The cousins ran "21" for the last three years of Prohibition, resorting to the usual tricks of the trade. "Jimmie" worked the front-door peephole. The door swung open if he knew a customer but stayed shut if he didn't. Sometimes callers presented a yellow card with Jack's initials signaling that it was okay for them to enter, but a "34" meant "Keep the stiff out."

Location was the key to the club's success. West 52nd Street was one of the "wettest" in the city. Kriendler once took Benchley on a mission to tally all the speaks on the block. They counted thirty-eight between Fifth and Sixth Avenues and had drinks in many of them. Kriendler and Berns lived in constant fear of raids, and didn't suffer one until *Daily Mirror* columnist Walter Winchell, who'd been barred, spilled the beans. Under a 1930 headline,

Inside the "21" Club barroom hang hundreds of items donated by customers. ◆ ◆ ◆

A PLACE NEVER RAIDED, JACK & CHARLIE'S AT 21 WEST FIFTY-SEC-
OND STREET, Winchell asked why agents had let "21" off easy. A raid
soon followed, in which ten employees were arrested. The owners
paid a small fine but got a boon in the headlines to follow, when Jack
and Charlie were called the "kings of imported liquor."

The last raid of "21" came in the summer of 1932, but agents
didn't find a single drop of alcohol after searching for most of the
day. The cousins had outfoxed Uncle Sam with an ingenious series
of secret doors and hidden rooms. They had constructed an elaborate
system both to ditch and to hide their stockpile. Behind the bar,
a switch sent all the bottles on a shelf crashing backward down a
brick-lined chute to the basement. The bottles broke, and the alcohol
flowed into a drain. Secret closets on the second and fourth floors
were hidden in walls behind secret doors; they could be opened only
with a coat hanger jammed into an electric locking system. One of
the fourth-floor vaults was ten feet long and six feet wide, but the
biggest of all the secret rooms was the wine cellar, built to hold two
thousand cases of wine. The room is now open to the public, and "21"
uses the space for private parties.

Throughout the Thirties, "21" was one of the most popular watering holes for the Vicious Circle. After Dorothy Parker married Alan Campbell in 1934, she and Benchley found themselves at "21" discussing their friendship. According to a biographer, Parker asked Benchley, "Why don't we get married right now?"

"What would we do with Alan?" Benchley asked.

"Send him to military school," Parker replied.

Ross and Broun were also regulars at "21." Broun, almost a daily visitor, liked to pull an odd stunt in the men's room. He stripped off his shirt and tossed it in the garbage, then asked the attendant to hurry up the street to buy him a new one. Later at the bar, Broun marveled that his laundry bills were exceedingly low. In November 1945, when Benchley died of a cerebral hemorrhage at age fifty-six, the memorial service was held at the club. A plaque to his memory simply says, "Robert Benchley—His Corner."

Today, "21" is about six times larger, has expanded next door, and has become one of the most famous restaurants in the United States.

## 4. Club Intime

Texas Guinan famously said, "You may mean all the world to your mother, but you're just a cover charge to me." She was an entrepreneur in an era that worshipped the successful speakeasy owner. She opened speaks such as the **300 Club at 151 West 54th Street,** where she was the hostess, and **Club Intime** just down the block, at **205 West 54th Street.** At the latter venue, on New Year's Eve, 1928, she charged a $20 cover (about $200 today). On the bill was a lisping Ruby Keeler, who married Al Jolson, and a brave show-girl who danced with a sleepy eight-foot boa constrictor wrapped around her shoulders. The club, just east of Broadway, was located

# Texas Guinan: The Queen Holds Court

During the Roaring Twenties, the queen of the nightclubs was Texas Guinan, one of New York's greatest celebrities. The brassy peroxide-blonde lived in the West Village at **17 West 8th Street.** She was to speakeasies what Ziegfeld was to *The Follies.*

The thrice-married Texas ran speakeasies and nightclubs, booked entertainers, and danced and sang herself. Her greeting—"Hello, suckers!"—was the most famous watchword of the era. The city adored her. The authorities less so: They raided and hauled her in so many times that she took to wearing a necklace made of tiny padlocks.

Born Mary Louise Cecilia Guinan, she hailed from Waco, Texas, where she learned to rope cows at fourteen. She came to New York before the war

"I would rather have a square inch of New York than all the rest of the world," said Texas Guinan. ◆ ◆ ◆

and starred in silent pictures as a charming cowgirl. She dabbled in other dubious activities until Prohibition, when she dived into the nightlife business with gusto, proving herself tough, friendly, and competent all at once. As Stanley Walker recalled, "[O]ther women might be superior to Texas as entertainers, but they lacked her imagination and her executive ability." Her venues were wildly successful. She could charge $10 a shot, plus a cover charge and extra for a floorshow. She looked down her nose at Broadway; Broun reported her quipping, "Anybody can put on a show with all those clothes. The trick is to put one on without any clothes at all." In one ten-month span it was rumored she raked in $700,000.

Guinan's home at 17 West 8th Street. ◆ ◆ ◆

In the sweltering summer of 1925 the city got too hot for Texas, so she opened a place in Valley Stream, Long Island. It became so popular so quickly that even Mayor Jimmy Walker dropped in. One of her biggest successes was a chorus girl revue called *Padlocks of 1927* featuring nearly nude dancers, in which Tex made her entrance on a white horse. In 1928 she was raided yet again and charged with selling liquor. As she was led out, she asked the orchestra to play "The Prisoner's Song." A month later she was acquitted after insisting that she was purely an entertainer and couldn't be tried for aiding and abetting a nuisance. She was driven home in an armored car.

The beginning of the end came in 1931 when she took her act and her girls to France. The French didn't want American showgirls to throw French dancing girls out of work, so they didn't let them off the boat. Tex returned to America and took her show on the road. She died of amoebic dysentery in 1933, a month before Repeal, and is buried in an enormous mausoleum in Calvary Cemetery in Queens.

After Prohibition began, Texas Guinan "became the best known person in New York's night life," according to Stanley Walker. Her speakeasy Club Intime has given way to Flûte, a Champagne lounge. ◆ ◆ ◆

in the basement of a large apartment house. Today, Flûte, a fantastic little Champagne lounge, has operated in the former speakeasy for almost twenty years.

## 5. THE EL FEY CLUB

Texas Guinan went into business with a notorious Hell's Kitchen criminal named Larry Fay, himself arrested forty-six times, in speaks such as the El Fey Club on West 45th Street. She put together *Fay's Follies* with girls wearing strings of beads—and little else. The beautiful chorines she found were known as Guinan Graduates.

Stanley Walker called Fay "the horse-faced racketeer" who went bankrupt with the club. "If a man wanted to throw away a lot of money, and a great many men appeared to be obsessed with this idea at the time, Fay's club was an almost perfect place to do it." A fellow speakeasy proprietor once took a few friends to Fay's place, and an evening of Champagne for the five ran to $1,300. "I was glad to pay. It was worth it," he told Walker. "I had a hell of a good time."

The end came swiftly. In 1927 a customs squad officer was beaten and stabbed outside the club. Soon after, the club was raided, and eighteen customers and staff were hauled off to jail in two police wagons. In 1932, Fay was murdered by a drunken doorman who shot him four times at his club.

## 6. THE SILVER SLIPPER CLUB

When notorious Hell's Kitchen mobster and thug Owen Madden was released from Sing Sing prison in 1923, he invested in speakeasies in a major way. Madden's friend and partner Bill Duffy, who also had a long rap sheet, opened the Silver Slipper Club in the Theater District in a block bubbling with speaks. Walker said clubs like the Silver Slipper "served good liquor, good food, fair entertainment, and kept a close eye on their joints to prevent crime—at any rate, crime of too flagrant a nature." But the club was constantly targeted; one federal agent repeatedly took his wife to the Silver Slipper for Champagne and supper to build a case, spending $35 for a quart of bubbly and a pint of rye. In late 1928, a federal judge ordered it pad-locked. By then Duffy had had enough of speakeasies, and became the manager of heavyweight champ Primo Carnera.

# What You'd Spend in a Speakeasy

Here are Twenties prices for a night out at a speakeasy. To estimate the cost in today's dollars, multiply all figures by ten.

- $1.00: a "good" mixed drink

- $1.00: ten Camel cigarettes in a special package

- $1.00: paper gardenia

- $1.00: small bottle of White Rock club soda

- $2.00: pitcher of water

- $4.50: four roses as a boutonnière

- $6.00: female company, or a "rag doll"

- $15.00: cover charge

Source: Stanley Walker, *The Night Club Era* (New York: Blue Ribbon Books, 1933)

## 7. MIDTOWN WEST SPEAKEASIES

Midtown Manhattan west of Broadway was a prime zone for speakeasies. Within walking distance of eighty theaters, scores of restaurants, and the subway, it contained an ocean of illegal alcohol. Notorious speakeasies of the late Twenties included the **Don Royal Club at 135 West 50th Street,** where seven arrests followed a 1929 raid. **The Art Club, 124 West 50th Street,** and the **Mimic Club (also known as Club Renault), 132 West 50th Street,** were raided often. An agent said he paid $1 a drink—and had thirteen of them—but that the liquor made his brain "keener" afterward at the Mimic. At the **Knight Club, 115 West 51st Street,** raids netted three men. **King's at 342 West 49th Street** and the **Charm Club at 137 West 51st Street** were both padlocked on the same night in 1928, the day Governor Al Smith won the Democratic nomination for the presidency.

## 8. POLLY ADLER'S BROTHEL

Polly Adler, a poor Russian immigrant who went from Brooklyn sweatshop worker to wealthy Park Avenue madam, ran New York's most notorious brothels. "I am one of those people who just can't help getting a kick out of life—even when it's a kick in the teeth," she said. She ran brothels all over the city, focusing mainly on the West Side of Manhattan. A few of her locations included **303 West 92nd Street** (1923), **411 West End Avenue** (1924), **57 West 58th Street** (1926), and **115 West 73rd Street** (1927). She had more than a dozen other locations as well. According to a *Forbes* article on the 1939 World's Fair, Adler set up shop on Central Park West for fairgoers.

Members of the Algonquin Round Table frequented her establishments in rented apartments scattered around the city. Among

Polly Adler called herself "a student of the human condition." ◆ ◆ ◆

Adler's many acquaintances were Benchley, Parker, and Kaufman. A notorious skirt-chaser, Kaufman had a charge account with her. Adler called Benchley "the kindest, warmest-hearted man in the world." He rented her place for lavish parties, bringing along Parker, politicians, and the literary crowd. At one party, a despondent prostitute jumped out an open window. After checking to make sure she was okay, Benchley kept the party rolling along.

Adler decked out her brothels in sumptuous

Adler ran a brothel from this building, 57 West 58th Street, in 1926. Today it's the Coronet, a condominium and apartment house. ◆ ◆ ◆

decor, with plush carpets, expensive furniture, paintings, and walls lined with books. Benchley and Parker, who became regulars in 1924, suggested titles for Adler's library. Patrons came for drinks, backgammon, and card games as much as for the prostitutes. Benchley and Parker frequented her brothel before a night of parties or after completing their Broadway duties. Benchley often spent the night there, and Adler claims in her autobiography, *A House Is Not a Home*, that he even did some of his magazine writing in the company of her girls. When she was in Hollywood, the pair had drinks at Chasen's. Adler had a twenty-five-year career in prostitution but got rich selling booze during Prohibition. Her all-night parties were regular functions, and "Going to Polly's?" was a catchphrase in town.

Adler was arrested seventeen times but never had a conviction until 1935. She spent thousands of dollars on bribes and kickbacks to the police but spent only twenty-four days in jail. Syndicated columnist O. O. McIntyre attended one of her trials, and had this to report:

> I had a close-up view of New York's notorious vice queen, Polly Adler, recently in court. She was the personification of the fabled glossy lady, dressed in Broadway-smart fashion, reeking of beauty parlor ministrations and a voice with that thin husk that suggests cigarettes, raw gin, and late hours. Invariably generous, their windup follows a set pattern— broke, friendless, a cell. Polly was no exception.

When World War II began, Adler knew the changing New York was no place for brothels like hers. By 1943 she was out of the oldest profession completely and retired to Los Angeles. She earned a college degree when she was almost fifty. Rinehart published her memoir in 1953, and the book launch party was held at "21." General manager Jerry Berns said, "Where else would she go? She had a business arrangement with us; we sold her whiskey, and if someone was looking for entertainment, he was referred to Miss Adler." The book sold more than two million copies before adaptations to screen and stage. The retired madam died at age sixty-two in Hollywood in 1962.

{9}

# WIT'S END

### Gone But Not Forgotten

*Death-bed promises should be broken as lightly as they are seriously made. The dead have no right to lay their clammy fingers upon the living.*

—EDNA FERBER

Members of the Algonquin Round Table either rushed up to fame, grabbed it by the lapels, and shook it, or they retreated to secluded towns or villages and hid out for the remainder of their careers. There was rarely any middle ground with the Vicious Circle. When fame came, they ran with it. But it scared the hell out of some of them.

When the Thirties began, the daily meeting of the Round Table ceased. Some of the members clung to their friendships; others moved along. Their fame grew exponentially. The group made a

Heywood Broun is buried in Hawthorne, New York, one hour north of the city. ◆ ◆ ◆

Margalo Gillmore, Marc Connelly, and Peggy Wood at the Algonquin in 1968. ◆ ◆ ◆

name for itself immediately after World War I, but some of its number didn't live to see the next one. The Round Table started dying off
in the Thirties, lost more in the Forties, and was gone for the most
part before Eisenhower took office. John V. A. Weaver went first, in
1938, and Margalo Gillmore closed the book in 1986. The *New York
Times* noted the passing of many on the front page, including F.P.A.,
Benchley, Broun, Connelly, Ferber, Harpo, George S. Kaufman,
Parker, Brock Pemberton, Ross, Sherwood, and Woollcott.

A few last, straggling meetings of the Vicious Circle took place over the years. First was the night in January 1943 that several went to the Algonquin after Woollcott's memorial service. It was a sad, brief gathering made gloomier for the old friends by snow and darkness.

Nearly two decades passed before another gathering occurred, and that one was not even at the Algonquin, but at the **Edison Hotel, 228 West 47th Street.** In February 1961 the American National Theatre and Academy hosted a gala to salute its president, Peggy Wood, on the occasion of her fiftieth anniversary in the theater. Celebrating with Wood were Connelly, Grant, Gillmore, Taylor, and Frank Case's daughter, Margaret. "There must be a gang such as ours somewhere today," Grant said at the party. "But, of course, times have changed. For one thing, the writers nowadays all marry cuties. In our day, writers were sometimes drawn to more intellectual girls."

The last true gathering of three founding members at the Algonquin took place in the Rose Room, in front of cameras, on the occasion of the publication of Connelly's memoirs in 1968. Gillmore and Wood stood beside him four decades after the legendary group had broken apart. This is how the other members of the group wrapped up their lives:

The twilight of **Franklin P. Adams's** life and career proved painfully sad. In a matter of a few years, he lost his newspaper job, radio show, and marriage. To make matters worse, F.P.A. probably suffered from undiagnosed dementia. Ross put his old army buddy on a lifetime stipend, which was honored after the editor's death. Adams's once-sharp memory failed him, and his personality, once just gruff, became harder to handle. When Esther Adams divorced him, she also sold the family house in Connecticut. F.P.A. had nowhere else to go, so he took a room at the Players Club. He was sixty-nine years old when he moved in, and his condition was deteriorating.

In 1951, his old friends hosted a wonderful tribute for him at the Players Club on the occasion of his seventieth birthday. Among the Round Tablers at the "pipe night" was Deems Taylor, whom F.P.A. had included in "The Conning Tower" almost forty-five years earlier. Another former contributor, Newman Levy, put together a special issue of Adams's column for the occasion, with material provided by Edna Ferber, Morrie Ryskind, Frank Sullivan, and E. B. White. F.P.A's oldest son, Anthony, attended and helped his father open the many gifts. A few years later, the old columnist's condition deteriorated to the degree where he couldn't live alone in the club any longer. In 1955 he was transferred to the **Lynwood Nursing Home at 306 West 102nd Street.** He lived on the second floor of the brownstone building for the last five years of his life. Aside from his ex-wife and children, he received almost no visitors.

He died on March 23, 1960, at the age of seventy-eight. His funeral took place at **Frank E. Campbell's, 1076 Madison Avenue.** Among the two hundred mourners who attended were Connelly, Ferber, Peggy Leech, Ogden Nash, John O'Hara, and Taylor. Connelly gave the eulogy, which read in part: "Rejoicing in the truth, he used mockery in a civilized, therapeutic way. His wit was never mean. He hated only the ugly. He stimulated more young writers in the Twenties and Thirties than any other person. He was a constant, brilliant light." Franklin P. Adams was cremated and interred in Westchester County.

Hardworking **Robert Benchley** stayed active until the end. In 1933, he began his first radio show, broadcast on CBS. He also appeared in forty-six movie shorts between 1928 and 1945. Columnist Sidney Carroll wrote in 1942, "The movies get a comedian and the literary muse seems destined to lose her most prodigal son for good. Literature lost out because so many people in Hollywood think Robert

Benchley looks much funnier than he writes. And they keep him busy looking at the cameras instead of writing for them." At the time, Benchley was on the Paramount lot making two forgettable films: *Out of the Frying Pan* and *Take a Letter, Darling*.

In his later years, near Grant's Tomb in Riverside Park, Benchley partook in an early-morning ritual at a small fence around a lonely grave with the inscription:

> *Erected to the memory*
> *of an amiable child*
> *St. Claire Pollock*
> *Died 15 July 1797*
> *in the fifth year of his age*

This monument, a hidden city secret, commemorates a boy who died nearby in 1797. Years later, when the city took over the land, planners respected the site and built the roadway around it. Benchley paid visits to it. ◆ ◆ ◆

Benchley is interred next to his wife on Nantucket Island. ◆ ◆ ◆

near **West 123rd Street and Riverside Drive.** Bringing a friend
with him to pay his respects, he got teary-eyed as he lamented his
own wasted life, cowardice, weakness, and failure. Benchley, to the
surprise of his companion, lamented that next to the Amiable Child,
his own life had been squandered. Diagnosed with cirrhosis of the
liver and high blood pressure, Benchley suffered from health problems exacerbated by his heavy drinking.

Throughout World War II Benchley kept up an extremely busy
pace in Hollywood. He lived in a bungalow in the Garden of Allah
and worked steadily in movies and radio. In late 1945, he returned to
New York for a break, but his health slid downhill. He collapsed in
his room in the **Royalton Hotel at 44 West 44th Street.** He died in
the Harkness Pavilion at the **Columbia University Medical Center
at 180 Fort Washington Avenue** on September 21, 1945. He was
fifty-six years old. Following a private service, his body was cremated

and the ashes given to his family. At the cemetery in Nantucket, however, the family discovered that the urn was empty. When the correct one was located, his remains were interred properly. His headstone, chosen by his son, Nat, was carved with his *New Yorker* byline. His wife is buried next to him.

Another Round Tabler who worked until the day he died (relatively) young was **Heywood Broun.** As one of the top columnists in the country, Broun helped to found the Newspaper Guild—the highly controversial first union for newspaper reporters and editors—in 1933, and served as its first president. He traveled the country to

In February 1940, 12,000 people attended a memorial for Broun at the Manhattan Center. Among the speakers were F.P.A., Mayor Fiorello La Guardia, Edna Ferber, and John L. Lewis. ◆ ◆ ◆

attend strikes, rallies, and press conferences, running his health into the ground with constant travel, work, and drinking. He spent a lot of his nights in the Manhattan speakeasies and saloons favored by newspaper reporters.

At home in Connecticut, he and Ruth Hale had an open marriage and lived separate lives, but her death in 1934 still crushed him. Broun had been seeing a chorus girl named Connie Madison, a young widow from Yonkers. Following Hale's death, he married Madison in January 1935 in the Municipal Building, with a ceremony later at St. Malachy's, also known as the **Actors' Chapel, at 239 West 49th Street.** The couple moved into Sabine Farm and renovated the house into such good shape that Eleanor Roosevelt came to a summertime picnic there in 1937. When Broun turned fifty, he wrote one of his best columns:

> At 50 I have more faith than I had before. People are better than I thought they were going to be—myself included. In mere physical exertion there may be some let-up. Instead of the daily constitutional of a hundred yards it will be 25 from now on. But at 50 I'm a better fighter than at 21. I'm more radical, and things which once were just sort of sentimental solace are now realities.

The former sportswriter never won a Pulitzer Prize, but he did achieve something better. On Christmas Eve, 1938, President Roosevelt, in his annual holiday radio address to the nation, read aloud one of Broun's columns to millions of listeners. It was a New Testament story, given an even more spiritual twist. Less than a year before he died, Broun began taking instruction from Monsignor Fulton Sheen and was baptized a Roman Catholic. "I have a strong premonition of death," Broun said to the priest.

In the fall of 1939 Broun came down with pneumonia and was taken to the Harkness Pavilion. He died on December 18 at age fifty-one. More than three thousand mourners packed the Cathedral of St. Patrick to attend his funeral mass. Monsignor Sheen delivered the eulogy. Most of the Round Table attended, as well as Mayor La Guardia and Newspaper Guild members. Broun was buried in Gate of Heaven Cemetery in Hawthorne, New York, not far from where Babe Ruth was later laid to rest.

*The Green Pastures* earned **Marc Connelly** a Pulitzer Prize, a gorgeous movie-star wife, and fifty years of dining-out stories. The wife didn't work out—he never mentions Madeline Hurlock Connelly, later Mrs. Robert E. Sherwood, in his 1968 autobiography—but the Pulitzer opened doors and set dinner tables for him. Connelly coasted on his 1930 fame for the rest of his life, and never accomplished much afterward. His collaborations with George S. Kaufman peaked during the Prohibition era before the partnership fizzled. In 1934, after the publication of a newly discovered novel that Charles Dickens had written for his children, Kaufman made a famous jab at his old writing partner: "Charles Dickens, dead, writes more than Marc Connelly alive." Connelly became a perennial Manhattan dinner party guest and Hamptons weekend houseguest.

In November 1980, Connelly celebrated his ninetieth birthday at City Hall at a party hosted by Mayor Ed Koch. Helen Hayes and Governor Hugh Carey paid tribute to his achievements. "I'm so old that I can withstand unearned compliments," Connelly said. "I'm grateful for being alive and for being a citizen of New York, which I think is the loveliest city in the world." Connelly died six weeks later, on December 21, 1980, while addressing Christmas cards in **St. Luke's Hospital at Amsterdam Avenue and 114th Street.** The turnout at the memorial service at Frank E. Campbell's was amazing.

John Guare, Ruth Gordon, David Mamet, and Stephen Sondheim attended, representing the theater world, old and new. Benchley's son, Nathaniel, delivered the eulogy. Connelly is interred in Kensico Cemetery, Valhalla, New York, in an unmarked grave.

It took two autobiographies for her to get her life story out, and when **Edna Ferber** was done, her life read like one of her bestsellers. "Life can't ever really defeat a writer who is in love with writing," she said, "for life itself is a writer's lover until death." When the final tally came in, she had written twelve novels, more than a hundred short stories, and collaborated on six plays. Most of her novels were bestsellers, her short stories sold for the highest fees going, and half of her shows succeeded at the box office. With the royalties from *Show Boat* and the James Dean epic *Giant*, Ferber lived her last years in style. Her last apartment was at **730 Park Avenue.** She died of cancer there on April 16, 1968. She was cremated, and her funeral was held, like so many others' of the group, at Frank E. Campbell's. Connelly and Richard Rodgers mourned along with a hundred others from the world of publishing and Broadway. Ferber once said that she hoped to be remembered as "a receptive and perceptive human being who has loved life and enjoyed living, and to whom the world owes exactly nothing."

The last surviving member of the Vicious Circle was **Margalo Gillmore,** who lived to see the space shuttle flights and a fellow actor in the White House. Gillmore stayed remarkably busy throughout her career, which spanned early Eugene O'Neill plays—with direction from the playwright himself—silent films, starring roles on Broadway, major Hollywood hits, and, finally, television. When she was sixty-seven, Houghton Mifflin published her autobiography, *Four Flights Up*, about growing up in Manhattan and breaking

Father and daughter buried together in Kensico Cemetery, Valhalla, New York. The symbol of Actors' Equity Association adorns their gravestone; both were early members. ◆ ◆ ◆

into acting. In it she wrote, "Chance plays a large part in an actor's life. Opportunity, even destiny, may hang on its light and gossamer thread." Gillmore died in her Upper East Side apartment on June 30, 1986, at the age of eighty-nine. She's interred next to her parents and husband in Kensico Cemetery.

F. Scott Fitzgerald attended parties at **Jane Grant's** home in Hell's Kitchen, but when he wrote "there are no second acts in American lives," he certainly didn't have his old friend in mind. After Grant and Ross split, the divorce spurred her to rethink her life. She went to China, Russia, and Germany in the years leading up to World War II, and filed stories for the *Times*. In 1939 she married a *Fortune* editor, William Harris, and split her time between a city apartment on Park Avenue and the couple's White Flower Farm in Litchfield, Connecticut. In 1950 she restarted the Lucy Stone League, a throwback to the first feminist movement of the Twenties. "Mrs. doesn't mean married," she told a reporter. "It means mistress of one's own affairs. The last definition of it given in Mr. Webster's dictionary gives it as the appellation for a wife."

In 1968, Reynal published her memoir, *Ross, The New Yorker and Me*, a warm look at the Round Table, her role in the birth of the magazine, and the bittersweet memories of watching her ex-husband succeed from afar. But Grant's real success came on the farm. She and Harris turned the little retail seed business into one of the most popular garden-supply firms in the Northeast. After her death, her husband sold the farm in northwest Connecticut. It still operates today and is wildly popular. One of the loveliest items the farm sells is the red and pink Jane Grant Rhododendron.

Grant died of cancer in her farmhouse on March 16, 1972. The *Times* callously buried her obituary on page 44, an ignoble tribute to a pioneer it called "the city room's first woman reporter."

None of the Vicious Circle had a gloomier end than **Ruth Hale.** At one time, she had a lively presence on the metropolitan scene, wrote for the best newspapers and magazines around, and hosted brilliant house parties on the Upper West Side with raconteur husband Heywood Broun. But as the Twenties drew to a close, she withdrew from life and spent her days alone at Sabine Farm in Stamford, Connecticut, living in a rural shack with almost no amenities, cutting herself off from old friends, and alienating Broun and their teenage son, Woodie.

By late 1933 she had been a recluse for almost five years. She went to Nogales, Mexico, and obtained a quiet divorce on the grounds that she and Broun had lived apart for more than five years. The news didn't come out in the papers until three months later. By then she was saying to friends, " 'Ruth Hale, spinster,' I like it quite well. I can go back to my friends as Ruth Hale. At least I won't have that god-awful tag, 'Mrs. Heywood Broun.' " But the divorce did little to calm her soul. She was forty-seven years old and not well. "After forty a woman is through," she told a friend. "I'm going to will myself to die." Her health deteriorated rapidly. She lost the

The farm where Ruth Hale retired to live, and eventually end her days. ◆ ◆ ◆

use of her legs, became weak, stopped eating, and refused medical care. On September 18, 1934, she lapsed into unconsciousness at Sabine Farm. Broun rushed her to **Doctors Hospital at 170 East End Avenue,** but it was too late.

Her son said later, "At her own wish she was cremated, and because she had not wanted one, there was no sort of memorial service. One day she was there and the next day she was gone." Hale's mother took her ashes home to Tennessee—without telling Broun or their son—and secretly buried her daughter's remains in the family plot in the Old Rogersville Presbyterian Cemetery under a headstone that sadly ignores all of her daughter's accomplishments. It omits her lifetime passion for independence and feminism:

*Ruth Hale*
*Daughter of Annie Riley and J. Richards Hale*
*And For 17 Years the Wife of Heywood Broun*

**Beatrice Kaufman** was the opposite of Ruth Hale in every way but one: Each tolerated her husband's numerous affairs. While the Kaufmans lived at various posh addresses around the city, George always held on to a rented apartment somewhere on West 73rd Street where he conducted his liaisons. Bea had her own young paramours to squire her around the city. For the last dozen years of her life, Bea worked in publishing as a reader and editor, and for Samuel Goldwyn as a script reader. But her real job was as Mrs. George S. Kaufman, supporting and encouraging him unconditionally. In the fall of 1945 she became sick, and after a brief illness she died on October 6, 1945, in their apartment at **410 Park Avenue.** She was fifty years old.

Friends made a condolence call to the apartment after her death. Ross wrote to Frank Sullivan, "After twenty words of monosyllables and three-word sentences widely spaced, George cut loose that Sunday and talked his head off. It was a very unusual thing." Kaufman wasn't a religious man, but he devoted himself to her memory. Each year on the anniversary of Bea's death, George honored her by lighting a yahrzeit candle, which burned for twenty-four hours in his bedroom.

Following his wife's death, **George S. Kaufman** went into a deep depression. Only after he met beautiful blonde British actress Leueen MacGrath in 1948 did he find life worth living again. She was thirty-four years old and had been married twice. He was fifty-nine, and after his second marriage, to her—held at his Barley Sheaf Farm the next year—Kaufman got back to work.

He played the curmudgeon as a panelist on CBS's *This Is Show Business* in 1949 and got into hot water for his wisecracks. He had one more stage hit, *The Solid Gold Cadillac*, which ran for 526 performances at the Belasco and Music Box theaters from 1953 to 1955. His collaborator was Howard Teichmann, a young playwright who worshipped Kaufman. Teichmann wrote the definitive biography of the man, which he admitted proved difficult: "I saw Kaufman almost daily for the last ten years of his life.... I thought I knew George S. Kaufman reasonably well. That was a mistake. I hardly knew him at all."

Not long after Kaufman's final success, he started showing signs of dementia, sitting in the lobby of his Park Avenue apartment in his bathrobe, for example. He had to quit playing card games because he couldn't remember what cards he had played.

His health deteriorated rapidly by 1960, and he cut his ties with his old friends and insulted others, such as Edna Ferber. Living alone at **1035 Park Avenue,** he suffered a series of strokes. He died on June 2, 1961, of heart failure. A memorial service was held at Frank Campbell's, which would be the location for many Round Table funerals. The *Times* said in a tribute the next day, "As writer, play doctor and director, he had a hand in the making of a joyous series of Broadway successes."

Of all the group, **Margaret Leech** may have had the greatest inner strength and drive to succeed in the face of hardship. Her first child died in infancy. A widow at age forty-five, she raised her daughter by herself, and outlived her. With her late husband's money she could have lived a life of leisure on the Upper East Side, but instead she worked as a biographical researcher and earned two Pulitzer prizes. She toiled alone in her apartment at **120 East End Avenue,** surrounded by her books and research materials. But in her seventies, she took particular delight in her grandchildren and in hosting cocktail parties. "I am sure about one thing," she said. "It's that I won't give a big all-purpose cocktail party. Living way over here on the East Side, I feel that if people make the effort to visit me, they should be fed."

Buried with her family and next to father-in-law, Joseph Pulitzer, Margaret Leech is interred in Woodlawn Cemetery. The stone carver originally misspelled her surname. ◆ ◆ ◆

In the Fifties, she devoted her time to *In the Days of William McKinley*, published in 1959. The *New York Times Book Review* called it a "first-rate study of a second-rate president." In the Sixties, she doted on her grandchildren by taking them to Broadway shows.

In the last years of her life, she moved to the fourth floor of **812 Fifth Avenue,** a nineteen-story cooperative, and worked even harder on her final book, about President Garfield. An accidental apartment fire in September 1972 caused second- and third-degree burns on her hands and feet. Two years later, she suffered a stroke and died in her apartment on February 24, 1974. She was eighty years old. Leech is interred at Woodlawn Cemetery in the Bronx, next to her husband and children in the beautiful Pulitzer family plot.

For a woman who marched in suffragette parades, rode circus elephants, and chased fire engines, **Neysa McMein's** last years were dull and painful. Her glamorous career as a magazine cover illustrator came to a screeching halt when editors switched to photography. She never recovered from losing her $30,000-per-year McCall's contract in 1938. Some of her wealthy friends took pity and asked her to paint their portraits, but her heart really wasn't in it. McMein spent her final years visiting with Woollcott at their Vermont lake house and seeing friends.

The last apartment McMein lived in was **131 East 66th Street.** In April 1942, while sleepwalking, the fifty-four-year-old fell down the stairs. She broke her back and spent months recovering at home. In the Forties, with no painting work, she turned to her other love, writing. She collaborated with Jane Grant on a movie script about a beautiful artist in her twenties, the most popular woman in town. They never completed it, nor was it ever produced. By the end of the decade McMein was so weak that moving around was difficult; unbeknownst to her, because her husband kept it from her, McMein had cancer. On May 12, 1949, she died at St. Luke's Hospital at age

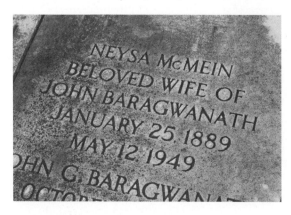

Neysa McMein is interred next to her husband in Rhinebeck, New York. ◆ ◆ ◆

sixty-one. Her funeral took place at Holy Trinity Episcopal Church. McMein is interred in Rhinebeck Cemetery in Dutchess County, New York, next to her husband, John Baragwanath.

When **Herman J. Mankiewicz** won his Oscar for writing *Citizen Kane*, he learned about the award on the radio. He was so convinced that he'd lose that he hadn't bothered to attend the ceremony. The 1941 award marked the high point of his career, and he slid downward thereafter. Throughout the Forties and early Fifties, he suffered from deep depression. He stayed in his bedroom on Tower Road in the Bel Air section of Los Angeles, secluded and in his bathrobe. When he did venture out, he got drunk and into car crashes. Eventually he had to give up gambling and drinking when his money ran out. At the end of his life he had so many debts that he had to sell his beloved library, among the best book collections in all of Los Angeles.

Mankiewicz suffered from liver and circulation problems, and in early 1953 was taken to Cedars of Lebanon Hospital and put into an oxygen tent. To his wife, Sara, he spoke his last words before slipping into a coma: "Well, that finishes everything I've to take care of before I go to meet my maker. Or in my case, should I say co-maker?" Mankiewicz died on March 6, 1953, at age fifty-five. He requested a nonreligious funeral without flowers. His remains were cremated, his ashes scattered.

In 1943 Herman Mankiewicz got into an auto accident in front of William Randolph Hearst's house in Los Angeles. Hearst played up the drunk-driving case in his newspaper chain. ◆ ◆ ◆

**Harpo Marx** made the journey from an Upper East Side tenement to a California mansion with a swimming pool, but his personality essentially remained the same throughout his life. From the moment he and his brothers became overnight sensations in 1924, and for the next forty years of his life, Marx made headlines and became a little more famous than he had been the day before.

After the Round Table split up, Harpo, Groucho, and Chico stayed busy making movies with Kaufman and Mankiewicz. Harpo visited Woollcott's home in Vermont and bought shares in it as a full partner. Harpo even made a solo trip to Russia in the Thirties (possibly as a spy for the US ambassador). As his fame grew, so did his circle of friends. He visited the French Riviera, and he socialized with Somerset Maugham, George Bernard Shaw, and Jack Benny. The Marx Brothers made their last film, *Love Happy*, in 1949. Groucho went into radio and then television, while Harpo and Chico played nightclubs. In the Fifties, Harpo performed one-man shows of his comedy routines and harp solos, but he spent most of his days in California with his four adopted children.

In 1959, Harpo announced that he was retiring from public life. Five years later, on September 28, 1964, he died in Mount Sinai Hospital in Hollywood following heart surgery. He was seventy years old. The final resting place of his remains is still something of a mystery. His body was cremated and supposedly interred at Forest Lawn Cemetery in Los Angeles, but popular legend has it that someone sprinkled him into a sand trap on the seventh hole of a golf course in Rancho Mirage, California.

In the Thirties, **William B. Murray** became a pioneer in the advertising business by packaging radio stars with advertisers to sell broadcast sponsorships. From his years in journalism he had developed incredible connections with Broadway stars and musicians. He joined the William Morris Agency just as radio was coming into its own, and he was there when television started. As head of the Radio and Television Department, he got rich representing Jimmy Durante, Al Jolson, and Fanny Brice. His personal life, however, was a shambles. Married three times, Murray moved to **333 East 57th Street.** His second wife, actress Ilka Chase, divorced him in 1946. Almost immediately he married a young interior decorator, Florence Smolen, who bore him twin boys.

Two years later, he died at Harkness Pavilion on March 10, 1949, at age fifty-nine. His son by his first marriage, William Jr., grew up to become a notable *New Yorker* staff writer and editor. In 2000, not long before his own death, William Murray *fils* wrote about growing up with a distant father, bisexual mother, and her lover, Janet Flanner.

After early triumphs, **Dorothy Parker** coasted on her fame in Hollywood with a modicum of success in the Thirties and Forties. She earned two Academy Award nominations, but she held screenwriting in such low regard that they meant little to her. She spent the Fifties in and out of love with her second and third husband, Alan Campbell, and shuttling between New York and Los Angeles. She settled into a routine of writing the occasional short story for *The New Yorker*, gratefully accepted and published by editor William Shawn. She wrote the odd book review for *Esquire*, which gave her a steady paycheck in addition to book royalties from the Viking Press. Her final major project was collaborating with Arnaud d'Usseau on *The Ladies of the Corridor*, a coruscating look at female loneliness that briefly ran at the Longacre Theatre in the fall of 1953.

She spent the rest of the Fifties living on the fringes of cultural attention, occasionally popping up to give an interview or to accept

In 1935 Parker visited
W. C. Fields on the set
of *David Copperfield*.
◆ ◆ ◆

Parker's cremains were interred in Baltimore outside the NAACP headquarters, twenty-one years after her death. ◆ ◆ ◆

an award. Unlike many of the group, she never wrote about herself late in life. Parker told friend Quentin Reynolds, "Rather than write my life story I would cut my throat with a dull knife." Occasionally the FBI sent agents to her door to check on the old radical, but she waved them off. She was called before an investigative committee, but nothing came of it. Alan Campbell killed himself in their West Hollywood house in June 1963, which sent Parker packing back to New York.

She settled into her apartment at the **Volney Hotel at 23 East 74th Street,** which she liked because there seemed to be as many small dogs as people in the building. During her last years, she battled an onslaught of illnesses and falls, but her mind remained as sharp as ever. Her heart gave out on June 7, 1967, when she was seventy-three years old.

Parker surprisingly left her estate to Martin Luther King Jr., a man she knew only through the media. Lillian Hellman, her longtime frenemy, was appointed to take care of Parker's affairs, but she made a miserable mess of it. Hellman pitched the contents of Parker's apartment, tossing all her papers and letters into the garbage.

After a brief funeral service at Frank E. Campbell's, Parker's cremains went unclaimed for nearly twenty years, sitting in a filing cabinet at the law office of her deceased attorney. In 1988, her remains were brought to Baltimore and interred in a small garden outside the headquarters of the National Association for the Advancement of Colored People.

When **Brock Pemberton** died on March 11, 1950, his old newspaper, the *Times*, said in his front-page obituary, "His success was in the traditional pattern of the small-town boy making good in the big city." His Kansas roots may have captured the paper's imagination, but once in New York, Pemberton carved out a career from low-paid drama critic to one of the most successful Broadway producers between the two world wars. His last success was also the biggest of his thirty-year stage career. He bankrolled and produced *Harvey*, which ran for 1,775 shows, from 1944 to 1949, and won the Pulitzer Prize. His marriage to Margaret McCoy Pemberton lasted for thirty-five years, although some believe he had an affair with actress-director Antoinette Perry, his longtime collaborator and friend.

In his sixties, Pemberton suffered from heart problems, but his success with *Harvey* invigorated him so much that he went on road company productions and even got into the cast. In the last week of his life he saw the show in Phoenix, then took a train back to his native state to see it in Topeka. He returned home to **455 East 51st Street** and died of a heart attack there. He was sixty-four years old. Pemberton's funeral took place at the Methodist Christ Church. The next year, the American Theatre Wing, which he had helped found, presented him with the first posthumous Antoinette Perry Award for Excellence in Theatre, the Tony.

**Murdock Pemberton** got the Vicious Circle going by inviting John Peter Toohey and Alexander Woollcott to visit the Algonquin Hotel together, which sums up the most important event in his life. Pemberton didn't have the grand success of his older brother, although he lived thirty years longer. His last two decades were rough. With no freelance writing work, he went back to *The New Yorker*, where he'd served as the first art critic, and took a job in the mailroom. His second wife, Frances, answered phones there for fourteen years. When she died in 1969, the *Times* flubbed the notice and printed that Murdock Pemberton had predeceased her. In 1974 Pemberton and Connelly went back to the Algonquin for the book launch party for a biography of Kaufman. Pemberton, age eighty-six at the time, said he took almost as much pride in founding the Round Table as he did in his children and grandchildren.

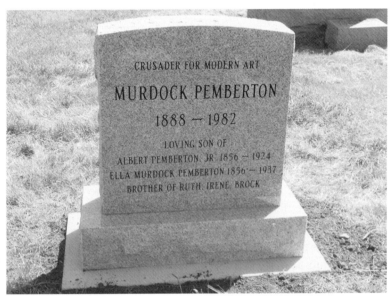

Cenotaph to Murdock Pemberton in Emporia, Kansas. ◆ ◆ ◆

On August 18, 1982, he died in his sleep at his Catskills home in Valatie, New York. He was ninety-four years old. William Shawn remembered him as "knowledgeable, intelligent, astute and idiomatic in his writing. As a man he was of some formality and dignity, and charm." Thirty years after his death, granddaughter Sally Pemberton wrote a meticulously researched book about his career and dedicated a beautiful cenotaph to him at Maplewood Memorial Lawn in his birthplace, Emporia, Kansas.

The last twenty years of **Harold Ross's** life weren't easy. He had chain-smoked since his teens, and the stresses of running *The New Yorker* gave him health problems that required him to take a series of absences from the office to recover from operations. His personal life had never gone smoothly, either: He had three failed marriages, but also a young daughter whom he adored. Ross did live long enough to mark an important milestone, the 1950 party to celebrate the twenty-fifth anniversary of the magazine he had launched with Jane Grant. (She skipped it.) "We'll go on as before—with luck," he told a reporter. Ross's luck ran out when he developed lung cancer. "I'm up here to end this thing, and it may end me, too," he said to his old friend Kaufman before surgery. "But that's better than going on this way. God bless you. I'm half under the anesthetic now."

Ross died on the operating table at New England Baptist Hospital in Boston on December 6, 1951. He was fifty-nine years old. Frank Campbell's hosted the memorial service, but whoever planned it wasn't expecting a crowd and booked a small chapel. Staff members, friends, and strangers packed the chapel and the entranceway. Another hundred souls spilled onto the sidewalk. As an usher passed Margaret Case, whom Ross had hired in the Thirties, she heard him say, "Goddammit! We got to get some *chairs* in here!" Ross's remains were cremated and given to his daughter. The old editor asked that his ashes be taken to the Rocky Mountains, where he was born, and sprinkled there.

By late 1937, **Arthur Samuels** was finished at *Harper's Bazaar* and had signed with radio network WOR to read scripts and produce programs. Like Woollcott, he turned from magazines to broadcasting. He and his wife lived at **50 East 72nd Street.** However, his radio career lasted only six months. On March 20, 1938, he died in Doctors Hospital after a brief illness at age forty-nine. His funeral was held at the former location of Frank E. Campbell's on Broadway and West 66th Street. He was cremated at Ferncliff Cemetery.

During World War II, **Robert E. Sherwood** became more politically active than in any other time of his life. In June 1940, he paid $20,000 for a full-page newspaper ad that read STOP HITLER NOW. Isolationists attacked his next play, *There Shall Be No Night*, about the Russian invasion of Finland, but it won him a Pulitzer Prize in 1941. When the United States declared war on Japan and Germany, he went to work in Washington. Sherwood became President Roosevelt's speechwriter, and went to Europe as director of the Office of War Information. His book *Roosevelt and Hopkins* won him his fourth Pulitzer in 1949. In 1950, he became a member of the National Academy of Arts and Letters.

Sherwood maintained a hectic work schedule in the Fifties. He moved to **25 Sutton Place South,** where he worked on his last play, *Small War in Manhattan*. He suffered from circulation problems, partly due to his height, and also from the gas attack he had suffered in World War I. On November 14, 1955, Sherwood died of heart failure at New York Hospital. He was fifty-nine years old. Most of the surviving members of the Vicious Circle attended his

funeral at **St. George's Episcopal Church at 209 East 16th Street.**
More than five hundred mourners heard a eulogy written by Maxwell Anderson and delivered by Alfred Lunt, which said, in part: "A
man's writings can contain only a part of him. Probably it's always
true that the man is bigger than the work he can leave behind. Let
us try to remember what we can of Bob and keep it vivid and clear.
While we have him in our minds he still moves among us and has
an influence on our lives."

**Laurence Stallings** had a tumultuous time in the Thirties. He
couldn't choose between literature and motion pictures. He and
Benchley could be spotted at "21" together, both men struggling
with the same issues of working for art or commerce. In 1934, Stallings became an editor of **Fox
Movietone News, offices at
460 West 54th Street,** and
lived at **50 East 77th Street.**
Anticipating the next world
war, Fox sent him to Ethiopia
in 1935 for what turned into a
two-year assignment. His four
cameramen recorded 50,000
feet of film as they waited for
Mussolini to invade, which he
did that year. Stallings filed
stories for the *New York Times*
on the conflict and then
returned home to America.
He abandoned his first wife
and two small daughters and
remarried in 1937.

Laurence Stallings was given a military burial and is
interred in San Diego. ◆ ◆ ◆

After America entered World War II, Stallings went back on active duty with the Marines in 1942. He served as an intelligence officer in the Pentagon and attained the rank of lieutenant colonel. Afterward, he returned to California to write screenplays, magazine articles, and books in Pacific Palisades. His health deteriorated, and doctors had to remove his other leg in 1963, the same year that Harper & Row published *The Doughboys*, his stirring account of World War I. Stallings died on February 28, 1968, at his home. He received a military burial with a US Marine Corps honor guard in Fort Rosecrans National Cemetery outside San Diego.

In 1951 **Donald Ogden Stewart** didn't know that he would become the Algonquin Round Table's own Philip Nolan. He and his second wife, noted communist Ella Winter, sailed from New York to London to produce a play. There, on a whim, they rented a house and decided to stay awhile. Unbeknownst to Stewart, the FBI had compiled a dossier of more than two thousand pages on him, tracking his left-wing activities. Agents had even followed him around New York and California. To date, some of his file still remains classified. While in England, his passport expired, and at the US Embassy he found that he was on a blacklist of "Red" Americans. The agency had an unwritten policy that the secretary of state could choose who could receive a passport, based on political beliefs. In this same way, singer Paul Robeson was denied a passport for more than seven years.

But Stewart fought it. In 1957 he sued in US federal court from London to reverse the ruling. Stewart won on the grounds that he didn't have to say whether he had had any communist connections for the previous fifteen years. The US Court of Appeals upheld the ruling.

However, the four-year dispute came as a Pyrrhic victory. Stewart never used the passport to return to America, and never saw New York again. He and Winter lived a quiet life in Hampstead. He did

DATE: 03-28-2007
CLASSIFIED BY 60324 AUC/BAW/STP/KMM
DECLASSIFY ON: 25X 3.3(1)
03-28-2032  ALL INFORMATION CONTAINED
            HEREIN IS UNCLASSIFIED EXCEPT
            WHERE SHOWN OTHERWISE

SECRET

# FEDERAL BUREAU OF INVESTIGATION

Form No. 1
THIS CASE ORIGINATED AT    NEW YORK                    NY  FILE NO.  100-83080   KK

| REPORT MADE AT | DATE WHEN MADE | PERIOD FOR WHICH MADE | REPORT MADE BY |
|---|---|---|---|
| NEW YORK | 11,18/47 | 10/21,31; 11/3,5-7/47 | |

| TITLE | CHARACTER OF CASE |
|---|---|
| DONALD OGDEN STEWART, was. "Don", "Dank", "David" | SECURITY MATTER - C |

b2
b7D
b7C
b6

SYNOPSIS OF FACTS:

Subject continues to reside at 8 East 10th Street, NYC and employed by MGM Studios as writer. Subject's play "How I Wonder" opened in NYC 9/30/47. Subject described as a Communist by [                    ] at House UnAmerican Activities Committee inquiry into Communist infiltration of movie industry. Investigation reflects subject has been a sponsor of numerous Communist front organizations and has associated with prominent Communists and Communist sympathizers. NY informants negative as to current Communist activities in NY area.

- C -

ALL INFORMATION CONTAINED
HEREIN IS UNCLASSIFIED EXCEPT
WHERE SHOWN OTHERWISE.

Classified by SP [           ]
Declassify on: OADR  8/18/87

REFERENCES:        Bureau file 100-18610.
Army information is unclassified      New York letter to Bureau on 1/17/47 in case
per their letter dated 9/30/88.       entitled "Ella Winter Stewart, was. Internal
NHC/PSR  6/1/90.                      Security R".

DETAILS:                [                              ] Confidential Informant
                        advised that the subject and his wife, ELLA
                        WINTER STEWART were residing at 8 East 10th Street,
                        New York City.

100-436938-10

| APPROVED AND FORWARDED | SPECIAL AGENT IN CHARGE | DO NOT WRITE IN THESE SPACES |
|---|---|---|

100-18610-117A

RECORDED
INDEXED
EX-103

COPIES OF THIS REPORT
5  Bureau
1  Los Angeles (100-    )(Info.)
1  Boston (100-14940)(Info.)
4  New York
   ( 1  NY 100-169378 )

F B I
21

COPIES DESTROYED

5 0 JAN 23 1949

little work, but old friends such as Ingrid Bergman, Charlie Chaplin, Katharine Hepburn, and James Thurber visited. On August 2, 1980, Stewart died of heart failure at his home at age eighty-five. His wife died of a stroke two days later. In his autobiography, published five years earlier, Stewart concluded: "My life has been for me a successful one, and in many ways a happy one. Can one ask more?" His remains were cremated.

After the demise of the *New York World* in 1931, **Frank Sullivan** moved home to Saratoga Springs and became the ultimate freelancer. In a small clapboard house shared with his sister at **135 Lincoln Avenue,** he turned out marvelous humor pieces for the rest of his career. "Once I visited New York for twenty years, but I wouldn't live there if you gave me Philadelphia," he wrote. "A small town is the place to live. I live in a small town 180 miles from New York, and

Frank Sullivan's returned to Saratoga Springs. He is interred in the local Roman Catholic cemetery with his family. ◆ ◆ ◆

while I would not say it has New York beat by a mile, I would put the distance at six furlongs."

Over the years, New Yorkers like Ross and Connelly visited Sullivan, who took them to the track, two blocks from his house, where he was treated like royalty. He picked up the nickname "The Sage of Saratoga," and worked until his early eighties. He wrote for *The New Yorker* for fifty years as well as the *Times* sports section, the *Saturday Evening Post*, and *Town & Country*, his work collected in half a dozen books. Sullivan suffered a series of falls in his home, and his health deteriorated. He died in Saratoga Hospital on February 19, 1976, at age eighty-three. He is buried in the family plot in St. Peter's Cemetery, in Saratoga Springs.

One of the more complex members of the group, **Deems Taylor** was the first successful American opera composer, and ranked among the first radio stars because of his authority and knowledge about classical music. He drew a national audience as a broadcaster, but he wanted to be known as a composer—despite the classical genre shrinking drastically year after year. Taylor received a measure of fame from narrating the Walt Disney classic *Fantasia*, but it wasn't enough professionally.

The multitalented composer had a messy personal life. He married and divorced three times. His third wife was nineteen years old when Taylor, then fifty-nine, met her. The marriage lasted for eight years. When he was older, his second wife, Mary

Deems Taylor and his third wife, Lucille Watson-Little, whom he married in 1945. ◆ ◆ ◆

Kennedy, came back into his life to help manage his affairs with their daughter, Joan.

In his sixties he turned to other pursuits. He served as president of the American Society of Composers, Authors, and Publishers (ASCAP) from 1942 to 1948. He even helped judge the Miss America pageant. In the last dozen years of his life, Taylor grew increasing feeble. He moved in with his daughter's family in 1963. He collapsed in May 1966 and was taken to the **Medical Arts Center Hospital at 57 West 57th Street,** built on the same spot where Neysa McMein's famous studio-salon and Dorothy Parker's apartment had been forty years before.

Taylor lingered in a coma until his death on July 3, 1966. He was eighty years old. At his funeral at Frank E. Campbell's, Marc Connelly and John O'Hara served as two of the pallbearers. Taylor's remains were taken to the Kensico Cemetery, twenty-five miles north of the city, in Valhalla. He is buried next to his nephew, William O. Davis.

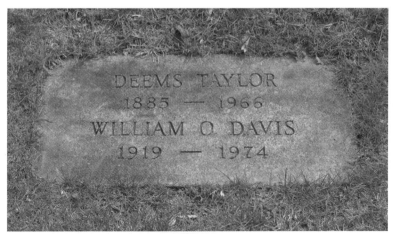

Taylor is buried in Kensico Cemetery in Valhalla, New York. ◆ ◆ ◆

In June 1919, publicity man **John Peter Toohey** uttered the sentence—"Why don't we do this every day?"—that bonded the group. A fun-loving soul, he played the straight man for the many gags and practical jokes at the table. From 1930 to 1942, he worked for producer Sam H. Harris on such hits as the Berlin-Hart *As Thousands Cheer* and the Kaufman-Hart smash, *The Man Who Came to Dinner.* Toohey's domain was the Music Box Theatre. His last credit was also a Kaufman and Hart show, *The Late George Apley,* which ran for almost four hundred performances, between 1944 and 1945. Toohey, who lived with his wife, Viola, at **43 Fifth Avenue,** died on November 8, 1946, at the **Beth Israel Hospital, First Avenue at East 16th Street.** He was sixty-seven years old. His funeral was held at the Actors' Chapel, **St. Malachy's Church, at 239 West 49th Street,** and he was buried at Gate of Heaven Cemetery in Pleasantville, Westchester County.

In *The New Yorker's* fourth issue, **David H. Wallace** made the "Talk of Town." On the eve of presenting a new play, Brock Pemberton was discussing a clothing sale and explaining that he had waited forty-five minutes to buy a new shirt. "What do you want to buy a new shirt for?" said Wallace. "You'll only lose it next week." The next year, the magazine reported that, after suffering through a well-attended concert by a diva whose voice wasn't what it used to be, Wallace remarked, "Well, her cash registers are still good."

Wallace had been a theatrical press agent and company manager for twenty years, and in the Thirties he went back to his professional origins: journalism. He wrote feature stories for the *Times* and freelance magazine articles. In 1945 he returned home to Syracuse and wrote about theater and art for the *Herald-Journal,* the same paper at which he'd worked more than thirty years earlier. Ten years later, after he developed a heart condition, he moved to Center Ossipee, New Hampshire. He died on June 15, 1955, at his home, at age sixty-six.

# When I'm All Through

*When I'm all through, and you got to get rid of me,*
*Don't go shootin' the bunk, or makin' prayers,*
*And all that stuff. And don't go stickin' me*
*Into no stuffy cemetery lot.*
*I want some room . . . I got to have room . . . I got to!*

*So if you really want to take the trouble,*
*You take what's left, and put it in a fire,*
*The hottest you can find—and let 'er burn!*
*Till I ain't only a handful of grey somethin'.*
*"Ashes to ashes"—ain't that a whole lot cleaner*
*Than "dust to dust"? You let old fire have me.*

*Then you just cut them ashes in four parts.*
*Take the first ashes to the side of a mountain,*
*Heave 'em up to the wind . . . I used to love*
*The way it's quiet and strong and big up there.*

*The second ashes, take 'em down to the ocean;*
*And when the waves come pilin' up the beach,*
*Scatter 'em where the green starts to get foamy.*
*They used to sing me songs about havin' nerve,*
*And never gettin' tired, or givin' in—*
*Let 'em run, and take me with 'em.*

*And the third part, you go out to the country,*
*Into some wide, long field, and spread 'em round.*
*Maybe they'll help the grass to climb a little.*
*I can remember how I used to roll,*
*And dig my face down in, and sniff and bite it,*
*And lay back on it, just a crazy kid,*
*And watch the clouds go skippin' over the sky,*
*And the bees, and the crazy birds, and everything*
*Would get so perfect I would want to cry.*

*Then they'll be one part left. You take that down*
*Where's they's the thickest crowds, right in the city.*
*And when nobody's lookin', give it a sling*
*Onto the sidewalk, underneath their feet.*
*The pore things, always hoofin' it along,*
*Somewheres, they don't know where, and I don't either.*
*Always lookin' for somethin'—wonder what?*
*I never got very near 'em. A person can't,*
*Even when you want to. Everybody's scared,*
*So scared, you know . . . so scared! But a bunch of ashes*
*Maybe might get real close to somebody once.*

*Just once . . .*

—John V. A. Weaver, published 1926 in *More in American*

H. L. Mencken said of poet **John V. A. Weaver**, who went to Hollywood in the Twenties, "His adventures there were full of the frustrations and disgusts that all other writers of any sense encounter. The movie moguls were never able to fathom so direct and candid, not to say tactless [a] man: they were used to much smoother and more politic fellows." Weaver had success with his free verse and moderate success with his novels, but Hollywood wanted him because he wrote "common speech" dialogue when talkies replaced the silents.

In the Thirties, Weaver was a fish out of water in Los Angeles. According to Mencken, "he liked the work, but in the end the malignant imbecility of the moguls wore him out." Weaver's 1924 marriage to Peggy Wood lasted, but they had frequent and lengthy separations. It's unclear when Weaver revealed that he had tuberculosis. When he went west, the condition worsened. In early 1938, his doctors sent him to Colorado Springs to recover while Wood was appearing in Noël Coward's *Operette* in London.

Weaver died on June 14, 1938, a month shy of turning forty-five. Five weeks later, Wood arrived in New York aboard the *Queen Mary*. At the dock she told the gathered reporters that she would honor her late husband's wishes expressed in "When I'm All Through." The four parts would be spread on a hill near their home in Stamford, a sunny field near South Stamford, and the ocean spot in Santa Monica, where they had shared happy times together. For the last part, she needed a busy avenue. "When I do, no one will see me," she said. "I will be alone."

For almost sixty years, **Peggy Wood** was an acting dynamo. In the Fifties, she did a one-woman show at her husband's alma mater, Hamilton College, in which she read his poetry and found it so thrilling that she took it on the road. She wrote two memoirs and numerous magazine articles about acting, but it was her last feature role that ensured her cinematic immortality. She costarred in *The Sound of Music* in 1965 as Mother Abbess. Another actress sang for her because she was seventy-two years old at the time, but she received an Oscar nomination for best supporting actress. Her last stage role came in 1967 in Westport, Connecticut, alongside Ethel Barrymore Colt in *A Madrigal of Shakespeare*. She visited Marc Connelly and Margalo Gillmore at the Algonquin in 1968 and told a reporter she wouldn't retire. "I have no idle hours. I'm in the theater."

In the early Seventies, Wood moved to a retirement home in Stamford. On March 18, 1978, she died of a cerebral hemorrhage at Stamford Hospital. She was eighty-six years old. Her memorial service, organized in part by Connelly, was held at the **Little Church around the Corner at 1 East 29th Street.** After Wood's death, her large collection of books was donated to a local library, which discovered that many were rare autographed first editions from the most famous writers of the twentieth century.

**Alexander Woollcott's** last several years weren't pleasant. He suffered constant pain from various ailments stemming from a lifetime of rich food and cigarettes. In 1930, his career revived when he joined CBS to host *The Town Crier* talk show, earning him $3,500 a week during the Depression, about $47,500 today. Woollcott divided his time between Manhattan for work and his lake house in Vermont for leisure. When World War II began, he took part in war bond drives with Dorothy Parker.

Woollcott had a serious falling-out with Ross, though, and the break was permanent. Ross had agreed that Wolcott Gibbs could write a multipart profile on Woollcott. Generally the rotund ex-critic didn't mind what people wrote about him, but he was unhappy with parts of it, and sent Ross a blistering note that ended their friendship, which had begun in the *Stars and Stripes* office in 1918. They never made peace.

On January 23, 1943, a few days after he turned fifty-six, Woollcott suffered a stroke during a live panel discussion. He was carried out of the CBS studios in his chair and brought to Roosevelt Hospital, but it was too late. A week later, a memorial service was held at Columbia University's McMillan Academy Theatre. Some two hundred mourners—including most of the living Round Table members—braved a snowstorm to journey to Morningside Heights to attend the brief tribute. Paul Robeson read Psalm 23, and Ruth Gordon gave a stirring eulogy. Following the program, several of the old friends met at the Algonquin, including Connelly, the Kaufmans, Leech, Marx, McMein, Parker, Ross, Sullivan, and Wood. Their enthusiasm waned without Woollcott's presence.

His remains were cremated, and a mix-up worthy of the Marx Brothers ensued. First, they were delivered incorrectly to his house

After a mix-up, Woollcott ended up at his alma mater, Hamilton College. ◆ ◆ ◆

One of the best places to live on the Hamilton campus is Woollcott House. ◆ ◆ ◆

on Lake Bomoseen, in Vermont. From there they were supposed to go to his alma mater in Clinton, New York, but they went to Hamilton, New York—home to Colgate University—thirty miles away. The ashes were sent from Colgate to Hamilton College, with a shipping charge of 67 cents due on receipt. Woollcott is interred in the Hamilton College cemetery not far from the campus theater. In 2000 the former Theta Delta Chi house was dedicated as the Alexander Woollcott House, and is now student housing.

## The Legacy

Nearly a hundred years after the Algonquin Round Table first started meeting, not a day goes by that today's media doesn't mention one of these thirty names—a backstabbing joke on a TV sitcom, a tired wisecrack used by a lazy sportswriter, or a reference point to anoint a new Kaufman, the new Parker, or someone as funny as Benchley. The Vicious Circle exerted its influence on its own era, but also on the generations that have followed. "As I got older, I resolved that I would one day try to write comedies for the theater," said Woody Allen, "and George S. Kaufman became an immediate role model." Maureen Dowd modeled herself on Dorothy Parker, her favorite New Yorker. Awards and scholarships commemorate many of the group: the Robert Benchley Society Award for humor writing, the John V. A. Weaver Award at Hamilton, an ASCAP writing award named for Deems Taylor, and the Heywood Broun Prize from the Newspaper Guild.

Ferber, Marx, McMein, and Parker all made it onto commemorative US postage stamps. Scores of books, TV shows, movies, songs, and plays have explored their lives and work. The films they created have gone into the Library of Congress to be preserved for all time. Screenwriting students look on Mankiewicz as a god, his script for *Citizen Kane* analyzed to the last comma. Every summer, Ferber's glorious *Giant* is playing on a drive-in movie screen somewhere in Texas, and a summer stock production of *Show Boat* is hitting the boards. *The Portable Dorothy Parker* has never gone out of print since the day Viking Press published it 1944.

Much of what F.P.A. wrote was ephemeral, but he did leave behind his *Diary*, now a goldmine of source material for researchers, and "Baseball's Sad Lexicon" made it into Cooperstown with the ballplayers it immortalized. Ross left behind a magazine that has become one of the most influential in the nation's history. Without it, we would have had no *Addams Family, The Lottery, Silent Spring, Brokeback Mountain,* or a thousand other cultural gems.

The Round Table came into existence when all points converged in one spot, in a perfect confluence of creativity, friendships, professional courtesy, and camaraderie. None of them really knew that

On the centennial of the Algonquin Hotel, in 2002, Natalie Ascencios was commissioned to create a new painting of the core group of the Round Table members. She chose, from left: Dorothy Parker, Robert Benchley, Franklin P. Adams, Robert E. Sherwood, Harpo Marx, Harold Ross, Alexander Woollcott, George S. Kaufman, and Heywood Broun. In the top right are playwrights Marc Connelly and Edna Ferber. The painting is the focal point of the Round Table Room and is near the spot where the friends gathered in the 1920s. ◆ ◆ ◆

their high-flying habits would mark them as legends for the rest of their lives. "I never have encountered a more hard-bitten crew," Ferber wrote in 1938. "But if they liked what you had done they did say so, publicly and whole-heartedly. Their standards were high, the vocabulary fluent, fresh, astringent and tough. Theirs was a tonic influence, one on the other, and all on the world of American letters." New York became a better place for their gatherings, its cultural landscape blessed with almost a century of influence after their time spent together in a hotel dining room.

# IMAGE CREDITS

Courtesy of the Algonquin Hotel: pp. 118, 122, 125 (top), and 251

Photos by the author: pp. 14, 21, 32, 46, 55 (both photos), 65, 67, 88, 93, 99, 139, 144, 149 (bottom right), 166, 168, 184, 187, 203, 209, 211, 215, 221, 226, 227, 240 (both photos), 242, and 254

Author's collection (public domain): pp. 2, 15, 20, 22, 23, 25, 27, 29, 38, 41, 42, 43, 48–49 (all photos), 50, 51, 58, 61, 63, 75, 81, 83, 87, 94, 97, 104, 106, 110, 121, 124, 125 (bottom), 142, 146, 151, 152, 154, 171, 192, 193, 202, 204, 212, 228, and 232

Anthony Adams, from the Estate of Franklin P. Adams: pp. 8 (left), 17, 18, 66, 79, 91, 100, 157, 181, and 217

Anita Aguilar: p. 126

Harry A. Atkins, from the Estate of Arthur Samuels: p. 73

Estate of Ben and Mary Bodne, courtesy of Barbara Anspach and Michael Colby: p. 112

Columbia University Graduate School of Journalism: p. 132

Noah Diamond (hotel illustration): p. 117

FBI (public domain): p. 239

Kate Pulitzer Freedberg, from the Estate of Margaret Leech: pp. 45 and 198

Getty Images (New York Daily News Archive): p. 208

Vincent Gong: p. 167

Paul Katcher: pp. 190 and 274 (top)

Permission Sally Pemberton, from the Estate of Murdock Pemberton: pp. 10, 66, 223, and 234

Photofest: pp. xiv, 53, 78, 102, 147, 160, 162, 164, 231, and 241

Public domain: pp. 5, 7, and 9

Nigel Quinney: p. 237

Frederick Rasmussen: p. 216

Courtesy of Scripps Networks, LLC: still photography on pp. ix and 274 (bottom)

The Shubert Archive: pp. 149 (top left) and 156

Errol Tony Soma, from the Estate of Tony Soma: pp. 195 and 196

Courtesy of the "21" Club: p. 200

University of Oregon: pp. 8 (right), 34, 36, 69, 176, and 178

US Library of Congress, Prints and Photographs Collection: pp. 31, 128, 129, 134, and 172

Waldorf Astoria New York: p. 56

Rebecca Weingarten: pp. 248 and 249

# Acknowledgments

On Dorothy Parker's birthday in 1999, I led my first walking tour, which stretched from the Upper West Side to the Algonquin Hotel. It was too warm for such an adventure, but, because we wound up in the Blue Bar, nobody complained. On that day I organized the Dorothy Parker Society, and I've been collecting stories, books, and photos about the Algonquin Round Table ever since. I also started meeting the descendants of the Vicious Circle and others associated with the hotel. Sharing some of the material and stories they've held for so many decades makes this book extra special to me.

Mrs. Parker's warm and friendly great-nieces—Nancy Arcaro, Susan Cotton, and Joan Grossman—were so pleased to talk about "Aunt Dot" and share scrapbooks and family anecdotes about the Rothschilds; I'm deeply grateful to them. I've spent many fantastic hours visiting with the last surviving son of a Round Table member, Anthony Adams, who inherited the wit and charm of his dad, F.P.A. Tony has been a wealth of information about the whole group, and I've cherished the time I've spent with him, talking about books and old cars. One of the best experiences I've ever had working on a book was riding in his classic 1932 Franklin sedan from his house in rural Connecticut to White Flower Farm, looking for Jane Grant's plants, and her ghost. The late Kate Pulitzer Freedberg, granddaughter of Margaret Leech, gave me a lot of wonderful information and material. Kate was so happy that someone was interested in her grandmother; it's bittersweet that she didn't get a chance to see the book. Thanks to Kate's brother, Nat, who has the spirit and *joie de vivre* of a Round Table member. Kenward Elmslie kindly chatted with me about the Pulitzer cousins and "Peggy" Leech.

Tony Adams, son of F.P.A., and I in Wallingford, Connecticut, 2013. ◆ ◆ ◆

Other family members who helped include the following: Harry Atkins, nephew of Arthur Samuels; Nat Benchley, grandson of Robert; and Sally Pemberton, granddaughter of Murdock. Lee Case Megna, great-granddaughter of Frank Case, inherited his graciousness and charm, and I thank her for meeting with me. Helen Beer and her brother, Paul Beer, the children of Mrs. Parker's caretakers, were tickled to talk about the old Bucks County farm, and saved many mementos from that era. Helen confirmed that Mrs. Parker liked to swim in the buff. Errol Tony Soma, grandson of the speakeasy owner, provided invaluable answers to my queries about his granddad and family.

Thanks to Debby Applegate, biographer of Polly Adler, one of my favorite Jazz Age characters. Once again, kudos to Susie Rachel Baker, the first Dorothy Parker fan I ever knew. Thanks to: Les Dunseith, who taught me how to research and ask questions; the late Gordon Ernst, top Benchley scholar, who cataloged his messy life; my photographer pals Anita Aguilar, Vincent Gong, and Paul Katcher, for once more helping me out in a pinch. Deirdre Greene and Nigel Quinney gave me my first big break in publishing in 2005. To the Robert Benchley Society members, Bill Hyder, Chris Morgan, Frederick Rasmussen, and president David Trumbull—I appreciate all the help and research into Benchley's life and times. To Dr. Robert Mielke, who taught me to write better. To biographer Marion Meade, for the kindness she showed me when I was starting out in the field. To the Sherlock Holmes of literary sleuthing, detection, and correction, Stuart Y. Silverstein, deep thanks. Thanks to Tom Tryniski for running and maintaining Old Fulton New York Post Cards. My parents, Don and Val Fitzpatrick, for support and love through all of my many projects.

The Algonquin Hotel has always bent over backward for me. The hotel has changed hands a few times, but management has always respected the past while looking toward the future. Nobody does that better than general manager Gary Budge. He oversaw the biggest changes to the hotel since it was constructed in 1902, and helped to institute the improvements and upgrades necessary to make it last another century. When he took me on a hard-hat tour in 2012 to see the guts of the building exposed during renovations, it left me in awe to see the care being given to the restoration of the structure. I was pleased to meet his successor, Manuela "Manny" Rappenecker, who immediately embraced the Algonquin lore and traditions. Special thanks to executive assistant Alice de Almeida, who always helps when I need it. She gave me a 1902 brick from the hotel after the renovation, which is more special to me than a seat from old Yankee Stadium. Alice manages the life and affairs of Matilda, a role she relishes and does with aplomb.

Thanks to Melissa Baker for the wonderful maps. For helping me locate the best imagery possible, thanks go to Ronald Mandelbaum at Photofest; Maryann Chach, Mark Swartz, and Sylvia Wang from the Shubert Archive; Kylene Sullivan of the "21" Club; Hamilton College graduate Rebecca Weingarten, who visited Aleck Woollcott's grave for me; Rosemary Morrow and Redux Pictures; Irena Choi Stern, Columbia University Graduate School of Journalism; Noah Diamond, the Marx Brothers' representative on this planet, who rendered the drawing of the Algonquin Hotel in a pinch.

I am deeply grateful to Anthony Melchiorri for taking the time to write the warm foreword to the book. Thanks to my editor, James Jayo, on our second run for the roses with the Twenties. To senior production editor Meredith Dias, for her herculean efforts to organize my mountain of words and boatload of images, I'll be sending you a bottle of Dorothy Parker gin. Lyons Press has been good to me, and I'm grateful for the courtesy and care they've shown.

Major thanks to my wife, Christina Hensler Fitzpatrick. She and I visited cemeteries, cocktail lounges, libraries, and strange towns together. She watched me write this book in four different apartments, and gave me the time to do it. I love you.

# FURTHER READING

Franklin P. Adams. *The Melancholy Lute: The Humorous Verse of Franklin P. Adams* (New York: Dover, 1962).

Polly Adler. *A House Is Not a Home* (New York: Rinehart, 1953).

Sally Ashley. *F.P.A.: The Life and Times of Franklin Pierce Adams* (New York: Beaufort Books, 1986).

Nat Benchley and Kevin C. Fitzpatrick, eds. *The Lost Algonquin Round Table* (New York: Donald Books, 2009).

Nathaniel Benchley. *Robert Benchley, A Biography* (New York: McGraw-Hill, 1955).

Joan T. Brittain. *Laurence Stallings* (Boston: Twayne, 1975).

Heywood Broun. *Seeing Things at Night* (New York: Harcourt, Brace, 1921).

Heywood Hale Broun. *Whose Little Boy Are You?* (New York: St. Martin's, 1983).

John Mason Brown. *The Worlds of Robert E. Sherwood: Mirror to His Times, 1896–1939* (New York: Harper & Row, 1962).

Joseph Bryan III. *Merry Gentlemen (and One Lady)* (New York: Atheneum, 1986).

Frank Case. *Tales of a Wayward Inn* (New York: Frederick A. Stokes Co., 1938).

Marc Connelly. *Voices Offstage: A Book of Memoirs* (New York: Holt, Rinehart and Winston, 1968).

Andrew Dolkart. *Guide to New York City Landmarks* (New York: John Wiley & Sons, 1998).

Robert E. Drennan. *The Algonquin Wits* (Secaucus, NJ: Citadel Press, 2002).

Edna Ferber. *A Peculiar Treasure* (New York: Doubleday, 1960).

Kevin C. Fitzpatrick. *A Journey into Dorothy Parker's New York* (Berkeley, CA: Roaring Forties Press, 2013).

———. *Under The Table: A Dorothy Parker Cocktail Guide* (Guilford, CT: Lyons Press, 2013).

James R. Gaines. *Wit's End: Days and Nights of the Algonquin Round Table* (New York: Harcourt, 1977).

Brian Gallagher. *Anything Goes: The Jazz Age Adventures of Neysa McMein and Her Extravagant Circle of Friends* (New York: Random House, 1987).

Margalo Gillmore. *Four Flights Up* (Boston: Houghton Mifflin, 1964).

Jane Grant. *Ross, "The New Yorker" and Me* (New York: Reynal, 1968).

Margaret Case Harriman. *The Vicious Circle: The Story of the Algonquin Round Table* (New York: Rinehart, 1950).

Susan Henry. *Anonymous in Their Own Names: Doris E. Fleischman, Ruth Hale, and Jane Grant* (Nashville: Vanderbilt University Press, 2012).

Gordon Kahn and Al Hirschfeld. *The Speakeasies of 1932* (New York: Applause Theatre & Cinema Books, 2004).

Beatrice Kaufman and Joseph Hennessey, eds. *The Letters of Alexander Woollcott* (New York: Viking Press, 1944).

Marilyn Kaytor. *"21": The Life and Times of New York's Favorite Club* (New York: Viking Adult, 1975).

Dale Kramer. *Heywood Broun: A Biographical Portrait* (New York: Current Books, 1949).

———. *Ross and "The New Yorker"* (Garden City, NY: Doubleday, 1951).

Thomas Kunkel. *Genius in Disguise: Harold Ross of "The New Yorker"* (New York: Random House, 1995).

Marion Meade. *Dorothy Parker: What Fresh Hell Is This?* (New York: Villard, 1988).

Richard Merryman. *Mank: The Wit, World, and Life of Herman Mankiewicz* (New York: William Morrow, 1978).

Herbert Mitgang. *Once Upon a Time in New York: Jimmy Walker, Franklin Roosevelt, and the Last Great Battle of the Jazz Age* (New York: Cooper Square Press, 2000).

Dorothy Parker. *The Portable Dorothy Parker* (New York: Penguin Books, 1944, 2006).

Dorothy Parker, Kevin C. Fitzpatrick, ed. *Dorothy Parker Complete Broadway, 1918–1923* (New York: Donald Books, 2014).

Dorothy Parker, Stuart Y. Silverstein, ed. *Not Much Fun: The Lost Poems of Dorothy Parker* (New York: Scribner, 2009).

James A. Pegolotti. *Deems Taylor: A Biography* (Boston: Northeastern University Press, 2003).

Sally Pemberton. *Portrait of Murdock Pemberton: The New Yorker's First Art Critic* (Chicago: Picture Book Press, 2011).

Donald Ogden Stewart. *By a Stroke of Luck! An Autobiography* (London: Paddington Press, 1975).

Frank Sullivan. *Through the Looking Glass* (New York: Doubleday, 1970).

Howard Teichmann. *George S. Kaufman: An Intimate Portrait* (New York: Atheneum, 1972).

———. *Smart Aleck: The Wit, World, and Life of Alexander Woollcott* (New York: William Morrow, 1976).

James Thurber. *The Years with Ross* (New York: Little, Brown, 1959).

Stanley Walker. *The Night Club Era* (Baltimore: The Johns Hopkins University Press, 1999).

Kevin Walsh. *Forgotten New York: Views of a Lost Metropolis* (New York: HarperCollins, 2006).

John V. A. Weaver. *In American: The Collected Poems of John V. A. Weaver* (New York: Alfred A. Knopf, 1939).

Peggy Wood. *How Young You Look: Memoirs of a Middle-Sized Actress* (New York: Farrar & Rinehart, 1941).

Ben Yagoda. *About Town: "The New Yorker" and the World It Made* (New York: Scribner, 2000).

### Internet Sites

Algonquin Hotel: AlgonquinHotel.com
Algonquin Round Table: AlgonquinRoundTable.org
Robert Benchley Society: RobertBenchley.org
Broadway Photographs: Broadway.cas.sc.edu
Kevin C. Fitzpatrick: FitzpatrickAuthor.com
Internet Broadway Database: ibdb.com
George S. Kaufman: GeorgeSKaufman.com
Margaret Leech: MargaretLeech.com
Old Fulton New York Post Cards: FultonHistory.com
Dorothy Parker Society: DorothyParker.com
Tony Soma: TheSpeakEasyKing.com
Travalanche: travsd.wordpress.com

# INDEX

*(Italicized page numbers indicate illustrations, and maps are noted with "m" following the page number.)*

# About the Author

**Kevin C. Fitzpatrick** is an independent historian who founded the Dorothy Parker Society in 1999. He is a graduate of Northeast Missouri State University and served in the US Marine Corps. After his hitch he entered journalism and worked in newspapers, magazines, advertising agencies, and television in New York. He is the author and editor of five books.

A Manhattan resident, Kevin is a licensed New York City Sightseeing Guide and has been leading walking tours for fifteen years. He is a frequent speaker at private clubs, libraries, and literary events. Visit fitzpatrickauthor.com.

**Anthony Melchiorri** has more than two decades of experience running hotels and was the general manager of the Algonquin Hotel from 2005 to 2010. He is the creator and host of *Hotel Impossible* on the Travel Channel.

His career started at the landmark Plaza Hotel. By age twenty-nine, he was general manager of the Lucerne Hotel. Seven years later, Anthony was appointed general manager of the Algonquin. He left to be senior vice president of the first Nickelodeon Hotel and Resort in Orlando. Anthony later joined Tishman Hotels as asset manager of the Westin Hotel in Times Square. A native New Yorker, Anthony has parlayed his skills to launch his own consulting company, Argeo Hospitality. Visit anthonymelchiorri.com.